© **West Midlands Police Museum**

The moral right of Corinne Brazier, Steve Rice and Helen Taylor on behalf of West Midlands Police Museum to be identified as the authors of this work has been asserted in accordance with the Copyright, Designs and Patents Act of 1988.

All rights are reserved. No part of this publication may be reproduced, stored in a retrieval system, or transmitted in any form or by any means, electronic, mechanical, photocopying, recording, or otherwise, without prior permission of the copyright owner.

Every effort has been made to trace and contact all copyright holders. The authors will be pleased to make good any omission or rectify any mistakes brought to their attention at the earliest opportunity.

First published in 2021. All pictures are taken from the West Midlands Police Museum archives or are free from copyright restrictions, unless otherwise stated.

Printed and published by Mapseeker Digital for the West Midlands Police Museum.

Contents

1. Foreword from Chief Superintendent Mike O'Hara – Commander of Coventry Central Neighbourhood Policing Unit 6
2. Introduction 7
3. Early Policing in Coventry 8
4. Coventry Police Museum 11
5. Chief Constables 12
6. Notorious Coventry Crimes and Prisoners 23
7. World War I 30
8. Coventry Bobbies 36
9. Coventry City Police's Female Officers 43
10. Sport and Recreation 49
11. World War II 52
12. Coventry Officers on the West Midlands Police Roll of Honour .. 70
13. Police Dogs 78
14. Vehicles 80
15. Diversity 87
16. Police Horses 91
17. Police Boxes 92
18. A Lifetime of Policing Coventry 95
19. Police Buildings 96
20. Police Forces of Coventry 102
21. Coventry City of Culture 103

1. Foreword

It is a privilege for me to be able to write a few words to introduce this book.

I have been the commander here in Coventry for over three years now, and it has been one of the best and most enjoyable times in my career. Coventry is a fantastic city with so much to offer!

I am very interested in the history of Coventry police. I have read some incredible accounts of trailblazing people, acts of bravery, innovation and people carving new paths. Looking back on these stories makes me feel incredibly proud of our history. These are the amazing people who paved the way and led us to where we are today, helping Coventry police develop and evolve over the years. It is important that we remember and celebrate them.

This book is fantastic opportunity to bring together and share those incredible stories. It is also a reminder that we are all the history of the future, so we must choose our actions carefully and make the most of the opportunities we have. To shape a better future for the people who follow in our footsteps.

Chief Superintendent Mike O'Hara

Commander of Coventry Neighbourhood Policing Unit

2. Introduction

Coventry has a very long and proud history of policing. It was one of the earliest police forces created in the West Midlands area and City of Culture year from 2021-2022 has given us the perfect opportunity to commemorate this history. Three different police forces have existed in this area: Coventry City Police from 1836 until 1969, then it became part of Warwickshire and Coventry Police, and then from 1974 it has been part of West Midlands Police which is the current police force covering the city today.

The hardest part of producing this book has been deciding what material should go in it, and what should be left out. It actually started as a booklet before we decided to just go for it and do a book instead!

There has been a police museum in Coventry since at least 1926, when it was referenced in the Coventry Evening Telegraph that two catapults confiscated from two young boys in Canley Lane would be added to the police museum. At this time it was an internally focussed collection of exhibits, not open to the public. In 1957, when the headquarters of the force moved from St Mary Street to a new purpose built station on Little Park Street, the force took the opportunity to relocate the museum to the new building and open it to the public.

Notoriously known as the Black Museum for many years, the museum at Coventry showed a glimpse into the darker side of policing and gave the public the chance to see what police officers had to deal with as part of their everyday work. Through creating a temporary museum in Hertford Street for City of Culture we have taken the opportunity to refresh the displays and show other aspects of policing in Coventry; such as the diversity of its recruits, the pioneer female, Black and Asian officers, some of the stories of bravery and heroism from the Second World War, among many other fascinating stories. We are grateful to everyone who has shared pictures and stories.

After City of Culture, the headquarters at Coventry will be changing again and there will no longer be a museum on the premises due to standardising the use of space within our remaining police buildings and making the most of every inch of the building for operational policing. Coventry will also be represented at the main West Midlands Police Museum at the Steelhouse Lane Lock-up in Birmingham, which covers the history of policing across the West Midlands, including Birmingham and the Black Country as well as Coventry and Solihull. We will continue to look for opportunities to work with partners to have displays of Coventry Policing in Coventry, and look to partake in events that give us the opportunity to share this history with the public.

Corinne Brazier, Steve Rice and Helen Taylor

West Midlands Police Museum

3. Early Policing in Coventry

Mr Bert Wilson, former special constable of Coventry City Police, spent a significant amount of time researching the history of policing in the area. In an article in 1971[1], he told how the records he had compiled (from hours spent in libraries and archives) spanned 770 years of the city's history. At that time 63-year-old Bert, a retired Corporation shops inspector, had served the special constabulary for over 32 years. The below information is taken from the information he provided in the article:

> *'The first mention was made of constables in the city in 1200 when Ranulf Blondvil, 6th Earl of Chester, forbade them to bring freemen into his castle at Coventry to plead a cause. The first record of an execution in Coventry was in 1239, when Ribaud, a priest, was hung, drawn and quartered.'*

As was common across medieval times, capital punishment was a sentence frequently given for a large number of offences:

> *'Other offenders were dealt with in more picturesque fashion. In 1485, several people charged with heresy* [beliefs contrary to those commonly held at the time] *were sentenced to carry faggots round Cheaping and Broadgate on Market Day. In 1525, 37 citizens were imprisoned and five had their ears nailed to the pillory* [similar to stocks] *for stealing the common box from St Mary's Hall. Four years later, it was decided that all persons found breaking down hedges or cutting down trees were to be put in the stocks for two days on bread and water...*
>
> *Mr Wilson explained: "At this time, many different forms of punishment were employed. Wrongdoers were imprisoned for comparatively minor offences, but other forms of punishment were also used. The basic idea was to expose the offender to the ridicule of his fellows and shame him into mending his ways. At the same time it provided an object lesson to deter others from doing the same.*
>
> *Nagging women for example, were punished by a few hours in the 'cuck' or ducking stool, over a pond or lake. The first record of one of these in Coventry was in 1423, when one was made and set up in Cheylesmore Green to 'punish chiders and scolders as the law wills'. Cheylesmore Green was the old name for the present day Greyfriars Green.*
>
> *In 1584 constables were instructed to take any persons found playing football in the streets to the common jail in Cuckoo Lane. It is not known whether the seven citizens who were jailed in 1639 for damaging the city walls were football fans, but they were freed during the same night by friends using clubs and iron bars. But it was not all torture and bread and water in the city jail. In 1432 the Leet Court ordered the jailer not to sell ale to those in prison.'*

One of the major disturbances during the past few hundred years occurred in 1800 when an invasion took place by a mob from Bedworth:

> *'They came to Coventry to raid the grain warehouses but were repelled by the city magistrates with the assistance of the 17th Dragoon Guards who were quartered in the city at the time.'*

A booklet written by retired Coventry officer Karen Crutchlow (nee Sheppard) outlines some of the criminal justice systems prior to the creation of the paid police force[2]. The watch system dates back

---

[1] Coventry Evening Telegraph, 25 June 1971
[2] True as Coventry Blue, Karen Sheppard

to the 1400s when the city was protected by defensive walls and gates. Citizens were required to perform watch duty and watchmen armed with staves, poleaxes and battle-axes with long wooden handles patrolled at night time to keep the peace. Alongside the night watch, a handful of unpaid parish constables were appointed each year to serve under the Head or High Constable and the Justices of the Peace. The watchmen worked out of the watch-house built in the early 1700s. It was square, three-storeys, with a dirt floor and cells in the four upper rooms. Stocks were based outside the front of the building. A model of the watch-house made by Bill Leeds has been in the Coventry Police Museum for years:

In 1832 Thomas Henry Prosser (a citizen and yeoman) was elected High Constable. He was an ex-Bow Street Runner. Special constables could also be sworn in as and when required in cases of public disorder to add manpower to the handful of constables and watchmen that Prosser would command.

It was not until 1836 that the Coventry City Police Force was established, with a strength of 23 men. The first Chief Constable and Superintendent of Police was Thomas Henry Prosser who served until June 1857. Their police station was a small building in Market Place. Coventry was one of the first provincial cities to create a paid police force. This meant they beat their neighbours in Birmingham by three years.

The initial wards covered by the fledgling force were Earl Street, Spon Street, Cross Cheaping, Bishop Street, Gosford Street and North Ward. Karen details the roles of the initial ranks under the superintendent who was in charge of the force:

Inspector: One inspector who was responsible for charge duties plus the general duties of a night constable or watch-house keeper – paid 16 shillings a week (16s).

Sergeant: One sergeant who was required to be on duty the same time as the constables at night. Expected to patrol the whole tour of duty, receive reports from his men and strictly enforce the duties & responsibilities required of them – paid 20 shillings a week (20s). At this time the sergeant was higher in rank than the inspector.

Constable: Twenty constables had to perform alternate day and night duties. 12 constables worked night duty 10pm until 6am, four constables worked a split shift of 9am – 3pm then 6pm until 10pm and four constables worked 6am to 9am followed by 3pm until 10pm. One constable remained at the station house as reserve. The age range of the constables was 22 to 35 years and they were paid 16 shillings a week (16s).

The force did not land peacefully with the members of the old watch system. In April 1836 the last watch-house keeper Thomas Gardiner and eight watchmen made a claim for compensation after being removed from their positions. After initially being rejected they were agreed by the Lords of the Treasury.

Bert's article continued:

> *'The stocks were removed from the old Market House and set up in front of the police station in 1840 and a surprising fact is that they were last used as late as 1861 to punish a woman for drunkenness.*
>
> *A new police station was formally opened in St. Mary Street in 1899, when the new Chief Constable Christopher Charsley began his duties in an appropriate manner, by personally arresting two thieves*
>
> *….*
>
> *In 1928 the first traffic lights were installed in Coventry at the junction of Barras Lane and Holyhead Road.'*

The article concludes by saying that Bert might document his findings in a booklet if he managed to find enough time whilst carrying out his duties as a special. We don't know if he ever did commit pen to paper, but if not, we hope that by including so much of his research here we can pay tribute to his heroic efforts to document the history of the police in Coventry.

4. Coventry Police Museum

In 1957, Coventry City Police relocated their headquarters from St Mary Street to new, purpose built premises on Little Park Street. The relocation also saw the opening of their historic police museum to the public for the first time, after previously only being accessible to police officers and staff.

Tony Rose has been the curator of the police museum at Coventry since 2000. Tony was a special constable from 1975 to 2000, and when he left the Special Constabulary he agreed to look after the Coventry Police Museum. Admittedly he only agreed to be a caretaker until a new person could be found, but 21 years later he is still going strong! Tony received a Chief Constable's Award in 2014 along with the curator of the main West Midlands Police Museum site in Sparkhill, Dave Cross.

Tony (left), Chief Constable Chris Simms and Dave Cross

Many thanks to all of the individuals who have kept the Coventry Police Museum going since it moved from St Mary Street in 1957 to the first floor at Little Park Street and eventually in the late 1960s to the basement of the building now known as Coventry Central Police Station.

5. Chief Constables

Thomas Prosser was initially appointed in charge of the policing of Coventry in 1832 – four years before the creation of Coventry City Police. At that point he was Head Constable and he became the Chief Constable and Superintendent of Police on 20 April 1836 upon creation of the new force. He remained in this post until 15 June 1857 when his resignation was accepted by the Watch Committee. In his obituary it was stated that Prosser had won the esteem of a large circle of friends, who would hear of his decease with sorrow. 'He was an efficient officer, and remarkable for the sobriety of his habits'.[3]

Thomas Skermer was Prosser's replacement. He had previously served with Liverpool Police. As well as Chief of Police, he was also the inspector in charge of weights and measures. His salary upon appointment was £40. In November 1861 he absconded following an investigation into his accounts. A photographic copy of his likeness was sent to London, Bristol, Southampton and other ports in an attempt to apprehend him. On 3 December 1861 in the Surrey Gazette under the headline 'Robbery by a Chief Superintendent' – an article describes how Skermer left the city taking with him the sum of £35 5s. 4d., money that belonged to the mayor, alderman and citizens. He was described as 38 years of age and a reward was offered for his apprehension. It hasn't been possible to find a record indicating he was ever arrested, so it would seem he was not seen in Coventry again.

This of course left the police with the issue of having a vacant chief of police post again – so Thomas Prosser was asked to return until they could fill the position. He remained until March 1862 when a new chief was appointed. One legacy from Skermer's brief reign was the introduction of detectives to the Coventry City Police. A Mr C Thompson (also from the Liverpool City Police) was appointed in 1858 – much to the annoyance of the local officers, who, judging from a letter sent to the Coventry Standard[4], were most put out:

> 'Sir,
>
> *Can you enable a few anxious enquirers to detect, whether the thieves who robbed several houses in this city last week and got away in broad daylight undetected, have since been detected by the detective-ness of the Liverpool detective, who was thought to be so detectable as to be worth £91 a year neither more nor less, for the purpose of detecting thieves in Coventry?*
>
> *Believing that some of our old officers at £1 a week, have shown greater detectivity, I think, in justice to them and to the ratepayers, we ought not to be saddled with an imported servant at 35s per week, without some special evidence of his superior detectiveability. For such a sum the city ought to get good detection.*
>
> *I am Sir, yours,*
>
> A DETECTOR'

A follow-up letter was sent a week later, clarifying that the detective was also paid £8 a year clothing allowance, and that *'when his detective scent induces him to go forth, his travelling expenses may become another charge.'*[5]

---

[3] Coventry Standard, 3 January 1879
[4] Coventry Standard, 25 June 1858
[5] Coventry Standard, 30 June 1858

John Norris served as Chief Constable from 1862 up to 1890. His main ambition was said to be improving the wellbeing of his men and the status of the force. It was stated in the Police and Fire Journal of 1 December 1880 that his vigilance had led to a 'marked decrease in the number of indictable offences'. One of John Norris's most notable achievements was the introduction of the police tricycle. Note the suppliers 'H J Norris' – it is unclear if they were related to the Chief Constable.

The Commissioner of the Metropolis had written to Norris during the late 1880s at the time of the Jack the Ripper murders to enquire as to the use of the police tricycle, and Norris wrote back to say that they had been most successful and that 'a smart constable in uniform on a good machine is rather an agreeable sight[6]'. It was reported that they were used regularly for officers serving summonses and also allowed inspectors to visit the officers on their respective beats frequently during a night shift. Known as 'the iron horse', it was reported in the local press that the first person to be apprehended using a tricycle was a thief who had absconded the scene of a crime in 1881. He had made off towards Solihull and Norris had sent an officer after him on a tricycle in plain clothes. The officer overtook the bewildered man almost eight miles out of the city, just before Meriden, and returned him to the station[7].

In 1890 **Alexander Grey** took over as Chief Constable of Coventry City Police. He served until 1899, his total length of service in the force being 22 years.

In 1899 Birmingham City Police's Inspector **Christopher Charsley** became the new Chief Constable of Coventry. He joined Birmingham City Police as a constable in 1885. Once settled in Birmingham in September 1886, Christopher, known as Charles, joined Small Heath Alliance (later Birmingham City Football Club) in an amateur capacity as a goalkeeper in the first of three spells for the club which finally ended in May 1894, and was later capped for England. A cartoon which appeared in a publication, probably The Sports Argus, stated Small Heath Alliance were so desperate to sign him in 1886 that Alf 'Inky' Jones, the club secretary, and Charlie Simms the half back, visited him at Ladywood Police Station, where he was in bed in his living quarters! He agreed to join but strictly on an amateur basis and not as a professional, full-time paid footballer (professionalism having only been allowed by the FA the previous year).

After progressing quickly through the ranks in Birmingham up to inspector, he then applied for the position of Chief Constable in Coventry – a post he commenced at only 34 years of age!

His new salary of £350 per annum was a huge leap from his salary as Chief Inspector in Birmingham where he was on £167.12 shillings per annum. In his letter of application outlining his career he stated: 'I have a genuine love for the service and have worked hard to master the details of each department.'

During Charsley's service, it became common practice for criminals to be identified by means of fingerprints. The Metropolitan Police kept records of criminals and their fingerprints in London in the

---

[6] Correspondence from John Norris, Metropolitan Police Heritage Centre
[7] South Wales Daily News, 22 June 1881

Habitual Criminals Registry Office. Charsley retired in 1918, making way for new Chief Constable William Imber.

Coventry City Police **c**1920s, *with Chief Constable William Imber front row centre. Note the backdrop of Coventry Cathedral before it was destroyed in enemy air raids during World War II.*

William Imber joined Coventry City Police as a constable in 1887, aged 21, after growing up in Taunton, Somerset. He was appointed detective in 1892. In 1894 he was promoted to sergeant and 1897, third class inspector. In 1904 he was promoted to chief inspector and continuing with his rapid promotion track, superintendent in 1908, when he left the detective department to take charge of the uniform branch. During his career Imber was commended numerous times for bravery, efficiency and effectiveness in detecting crime.

William Imber – believed to be just after he received his Kings Police Medal, courtesy of Ed Matthews

He was an accomplished detective by all accounts commended numerous times by the Watch Committee – one of his most famous cases was that of the Harlesden (London) 'Trunk Murderer', Charles Devereaux, who fled London after murdering his wife and two infant children and stuffing their bodies into a tin trunk which he then deposited with a removals company for storage (1905). According to the Police Review, 'it was upon Mr Imber's final report that the police in London forced open the trunk and found the remains of Devereaux's victims.' Imber then arrested Deveraux in Coventry at his place of employment who was later hanged for his crimes. His obituary in a local paper also reported 'one of the smartest pieces of work which Mr Imber did was to clear up the Coventry Post Office mystery a few years ago. The office had been robbed of about £2000 and the recovery of the money proved a baffling problem. The police visited the house of a suspect and searched without avail. Imber made a return visit, however, and, noticing in one of the rooms a piece of plastering that looked new, he was led to the discovery of the hoard, which was concealed in small tin boxes in the plasterwork of the staircase.'[8] He was also a key figure in policing the visit of a Chinese minister in 1909, when his work tracking several Birmingham criminals led to a vicious assault upon him whereby he almost lost consciousness, but still succeeded in making arrests. In 1918 after recently being appointed Deputy Chief Constable of the force he had worked his way up, Imber was appointed Acting Chief Constable upon the resignation of Christopher Charsley. He was confirmed in this post by the Watch Committee in February 1919 and was subsequently admitted to the United Grand Lodge of England Freemasons. In 1926 he was the recipient of the Kings Police Medal. In April 1927 Imber retired, after 40 years' service with the city force. The Coventry Evening Telegraph of 22 April 1927 includes an article on the farewell presentation for the departing Chief. It was said that during his 40 years with Coventry City Police, whilst working his way up from constable to the highest ranking position, he had earned the respect and esteem of people in all spheres of life. He was also described as an inspiration to all the members of the force. Several of the speeches included mention of people from all walks of life feeling they could go to the Chief Constable with their problems and he would give them sound advice. In his return speech, Imber described how the force had only 46 officers when

---

[8] Coventry Herald, December 16 & 17 1927

he joined, and he was paid a meagre 18s a week, being left on his own to work a night shift by his third night on the job.

He said when he joined, Chief Constable Norris said to him *'Young man, I like your manner and appearance very much indeed, but let me tell you this, for the first six months you will wish you had never seen or heard of the police service, but after that time, if you survive, I shall not be able to kick you away if I want to.'* Imber stated he found the old Chief's words to be quite true! At the time he left, the Coventry City Police establishment was 182.

Imber was a keen horseman and is in the centre of the below picture.

The next Chief Constable was **Captain Stanley Albert Hector**, who served as Chief from 1927 to 1946, overseeing policing of Coventry during the Blitz. During his time in office he introduced police boxes to Coventry and also increased the establishment of the force from 182 to 322. During World War I he served in the Army and gained the rank of captain, however he joined the police service as a constable.

During his career he received the King's Police Medal, O.B.E. and was an Officer of the Order of St John of Jerusalem. He also received the R.S.P.C.A.'s silver meritorious medal.

Captain Hector also introduced policewomen into the city in 1938, after the suggestion had come up numerous times previously at the Watch Committee and been dismissed.

He had to oversee complex policing operations during World War II including increasing the establishment of the special constabulary, delivering training in wartime duties, recruitment of police war reserve constables, women's auxiliary corps and police messengers. He had to deal with the bombing of the force's HQ at St Mary Street and the loss of 10 officers whilst serving with the Armed Forces, and a further 17 in Coventry (including two police messengers and numerous special constables).

Captain Stanley Albert Hector

Captain Hector can be seen below at the front of the party escorting the Prince of Wales around Coventry in his visit to the city in 1935 (pic courtesy of Geoff Bowers):

Following the retirement of Captain Hector, the new **Chief Constable George Jackson** was appointed in September 1946. Having joined Hull City Police in 1923 following a brief spell in the Merchant Navy (including being shipwrecked on his first voyage!), he had since reached the rank of superintendent by 1939 when he left Hull to become Chief Constable of Newcastle-under-Lyme in 1943. In May 1945 he was released to become the first Commandant of the first official Police Training Centre for at Ryton-on-Dunsmore, just outside of Coventry. When this post was taken up he had one clerk and not even a sheet of paper by way of equipment! Captain Hector rendered great assistance and offered the whole of the Coventry Police's support to Mr Jackson. The Ryton training facility was the test pilot for the new national training scheme and it proved a huge success and became the model for which other sites around the country were based. One of the biggest centres in the country, it had capacity for 400 students, including policewomen. It was this work for which he was awarded the O.B.E. in the King's birthday honours list in 1945.

Pic credit: Coventry Evening Telegraph 19 September 1946, ©Reach PLC

The next and final Chief Constable of Coventry City Police, was **Edward William Cowpe Pendleton** who took up the mantle in 1948 until the force was merged with Warwickshire Constabulary in 1969. Here he is, pictured as a young PC.

It was reported that more than 300 policemen, retired policemen, civilian staff and special constables gathered in the police assembly hall to see Mr Pendleton off upon his retirement in March 1969[9]. Amongst the retired policemen were some men who had seen service prior to the First World War. Mr Pendleton served 42 years of police service, 21 of them as Chief Constable. After taking charge of the force only three years after the end of World War II, when the city and the force had suffered extreme devastation, he had overseen the move to the new headquarters at Little Park Street and made the decision to open the police museum up to the public in 1957. He had also been the Chief Constable that Britain's first Asian officer Mohammed Yusuf Daar saw on TV talking about non-white officers finally being allowed to join the service, which convinced him to make history by signing up to join the Coventry City Police the following day.

In the Coventry Express of 30 July 1965, Mr Pendleton made the famous prediction that by the year 2000, hidden cameras, helicopters and high frequency pocket radios would all be part of the policeman's daily life

---

[9] Coventry Evening Telegraph, 29 March 1969

in Coventry. Some of the very significant changes overseen by this Chief Constable included the introduction of police dogs, personal radios and panda cars.

It was stated at the event on the 29 March, the last in a long line of presentation events for the outgoing Chief, by Assistant Chief Constable S Porter that:

'I doubt if in the history of the police force there has been an officer who has shown so much devotion to duty as you have. You have achieved a status that many of us chase all our lives but never attain. You have established a reputation which none of us will ever gain.'

It was claimed many men of lesser character would have opted out during the difficult transition period following the move to merge the force with Warwickshire, but Mr Pendleton stuck with the force and saw it through. In his response, Mr Pendleton stated 'It is alright being the leader, but it is the team that matters.'

Mr Edward Pendleton O.B.E. B.E.M. Q.P.M.

6. Notorious Coventry Crimes and Prisoners

Mary Ball

Mary Ball is infamous for being the last person to be hung in Coventry, and the last person publicly executed in the city. Her crime was the murder of her husband Thomas Ball. They had been married for 12 years and they had one child. Mary had given birth to six children in total, but she had lost five as was common in this time period. There were reports of the couple frequently arguing, that Thomas was a jealous man and there was at least one proven case where Thomas had beaten Mary[10]. It was also implied that he regularly cheated on her with other women.

Mary was accused of murdering her husband by poisoning him with arsenic. The drug was widely available at chemists at the time and was unregulated. It was used to get rid of pests and was even used as a food colorant. On 4 May 1849 Mary and a friend went shopping and at a chemist Mary bought a pennyworth of arsenic to kill bed bugs[11].

Witnesses to the case gave conflicting accounts; one stating that Mary had told them she had poisoned her husband on purpose. Another witness stated that Thomas had complained of feeling ill after a fishing trip. Mary had suggested that he take some salts to relieve his illness. Perhaps he had taken the poison by accident? Initially being recorded as death by natural causes, Mary gave differing accounts to police officers when later questioned and quickly came under suspicion, leading to her arrest and a post mortem which revealed the arsenic.

The jury initially returned a verdict of guilty and asked that mercy be shown and that she be imprisoned rather than put to death. The Judge asked on what grounds and the foreman stated some of the members of the jury were not satisfied with some of the evidence. The Judge promptly sent them back to re-examine the evidence and when they returned with a verdict of guilty he donned the black cap and sentenced her to death.

She was said to have been very anxious in the days leading up to her fate - asking God to have mercy on her soul and worrying about the fate of her only surviving child. The gallows were set up in Cuckoo Lane in the city centre for Mary Ball's hanging and 20,000 people crowded around to watch. It was said that Coventry had seldom seen more people present than were there to watch the execution.

In an interesting twist to the tale - the gaol Chaplain - Rev Richard Chapman - was removed from post a couple of months later, following allegations he burned Mary Ball's hand with a candle upon visiting her at the gaol. It was reported that he held her hand over the candle (one witness stated for two minutes) whilst the prisoner struggled to take her hand back. He admitted that he did indeed hold her hand over a candle, and did so not to be cruel, but to give her an understanding of what the torments of hell might be like. The following day Mary made a full confession to the governor of the gaol.[12]

Looking at the case with modern eyes, it is very easy to see Mary as a victim of domestic violence. A woman who had had enough and one day snapped. Do you think her punishment was justified?

Below is a contemporary poster about the trail and execution of Mary Ball.

---

[10] https://www.theherbert.org/news/147/tales_from_the_archives_mary_ball_murderer
[11] Ibid.
[12] Ibid.

THE LIFE, TRIAL, AND AWFUL
EXECUTION
OF
MARY BALL,
FOR THE WILFUL MURDER OF HER HUSBAND,
AT NUNEATON IN 1849.

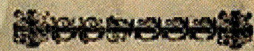

A COPY OF VERSES.

O listen to my fate of woe,
A tale both sad and true ;
'Twill bid the tear of grief to flow,
It asks a tear from you.
Now all human help is vain
Assistance comes to late,
Who will simpathy restrain
O'er my unhappy fate.

In Nuneaton town I lived, alas,
In my younger days was free,
From evil thoughts, or bad designs,
O Lord look down on me.
Arrived at age, I married got,
To a youth I lov'd most dear,
I little thought at that time
To him I'd prove severe.

By satan tempted from a path,
In which I long had trod,
I soon forgot my marriage vows,
And passed by the house of God.
When once my mind was led away,
I hardened soon became,
The crime that I did then commit,
Alone I am to blame.

Condemned to die upon a tree,
For Murder base and foul,
Kind christians pity my sad fate,
And pray for my poor soul.
I own I did the dreadful crime
And ought to be hanged to,
For killing of a husband dear,
Who was always kind to me.

Farewell my child, a long farewell,
My blessings rest on thee,
I hope no one will you reproach,
For the crime that's been done by me.
Father, Mother, and relations all,
I bid you now adieu,
My offended God, I soon shall see,
And my dear husband too.

The bell now tolls, O solemn sound,
It bids my guilty trespass,
What thousands come to see me die,
I hope they will beware.
And not their church and God neglect,
But for mercy loudly call
Think on the day for mercy pray
And pity MARY BALL.

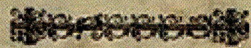

THE TRIAL.

This interesting Trial, which has attracted so much attention among the Inhabitants of Coventry, Nuneaton, Hinckley, Atherstone, and surrounding neighbourhood, came off on Saturday week, at our Criminal Court.

At an early hour in the morning the Court was literally besieged by persons anxious to gain admittance, and before the arrival of Justice Coleridge, the Court was crowded to suffocation. After his Lordship had taken his seat the prisoner was placed at the Bar; she appeared much agitated, and gazed round, seemingly longing for the final issue. Silence being proclaimed, the indictment was read over charging her with the Wilful Murder of her own husband, Thomas Ball, by poison, on the 18th day of May last, in the parish of Nuneaton, in the County of Warwick. On the usual question been put, she with a tremulous voice, pleaded not Guilty.

Mr. Hayes and Mr. Meller, counsel for the prosecution Mr. Miller, a the counsel for the Prisoner.

The first witness called was Joseph Petty, who went out with the deceased, Thomas Ball, in the morning of the 18th of May, to go a fishing, and returned home with him about 4 o'clock in the afternoon. At 6 o'clock the same evening prisoner came to his house and said " Tom's very bad." I went to see him the next morning, when he said he could not speak, was very sick, and had a pain in his bowels. Prisoner was in the room crying. I saw deceased again that evening, and again at twelve o'clock at night, when he still continued very ill ; his arms were numbed and cold, and he said he should die. Prisoner came to witness at 2 o'clock in the morning and said I want you to come for Tom's dead. They had been married 12 years, had 6 children, 5 of whom had died.

John Prouse, a Surgeon, made a post-mortem examination ; and Mr. Shaw tested the contents of the stomach and found arsenic therein.

Selina Ryland proved she had known prisoner and her husband to quarrel. He was jealous of her and beat her once and she said if he did so again she would poison him.

Mary Bishop, had also heard prisoner use threats against the life of her husband.

Elizabeth Richardson gave evidence that she went with prisoner on the 4th of May to a chemists shop to buy a pennyworth of arsenic, which she said was to poison bugs with. On the Sunday after deceased died prisoner came into her house and said it was a good job he was gone.

When taken by Vernon the constable, she told him she had used arsenic to poison the bugs; she afterwards told the same constable that she put a little of the arsenic in a sugar paper and laid it on a shelf in the pantry near some salts, and her husband must have taken it by mistake. Ann Hopkins who went to look at deceased after he was dead, stated that prisoner told her she mixed the bit of arsenic with some salts and gave it her husband, and then afterwards gave him some gruel.

A number of other witnesses were examined and cross examined ; but the above are the chief facts in the case. Mr. Miller addressed the Jury in a long speech in favour of the prisoner.

The summing up occupied 1 hour and twenty-five minutes. The jury retired at twenty-five minutes to seven. At ten minutes past eight they had agreed to a verdict of guilty, with a recommendation for mercy. His lordship asked, upon what grounds ? The foreman replied that some of the jury were not quite satisfied with part of the evidence. The judge told them they must reconsider their verdict. The Jury turned round, and immediately returned a verdict of guilty. The judge then put on the black cap, upon seeing which the prisoner shrieked out, begged for mercy, and declared she was innocent.

Prisoner at the bar, you have been found guilty, by a Jury of your country of the horrid crime of Murder, and it is one of the deepest die; the man whom you accompanied to the altar of God, and vowed to cherish, you have with deadly malice deprived of life ; it is said in the Holy writings, who so sheddeth man's blood by man shall his blood be shed; the Almighty has caused, through the all seeing eye of providence, the horrid deed to be brought to light, your days in this world are numbered. I cannot hold out to you the least hopes of mercy ; still the law allows you more time than you allowed your victim, whom you sent to his last abode with all his sins on his head, you have now time to repent and I hope you will make good use of the time allowed you in praying to that great God whom you have so grosly offended, it only remains for me to pass on you the sentence ; not my sentence, but the sentence of the Court, which is, that you be taken from hence to the place from whence you came, from there to the place of Execution, there to be hanged by the neck till your body be dead, your body afterwards buried within the precincts of the gaol, and may the Lord have mercy on your Soul. She appeared much affected on hearing the Sentence, and was lead from the bar.

Her uncle and aunt, two sisters, and brother-in-law visited her on Tuesday between the hours of 1 and 2, the meeting to all was very affecting. The interview was short,

lasting about half-an-hour ; during which time she manifested every sign of penetance and contrition ; not attempting to deny the henousness of her offence. She has taken very little refreshment during the present week, and appears resigned to her fate. She has made a confession of her guilt.

EXECUTION.

The awful execution of Mary Ball took place this morning. Many thousands of persons began to assemble in Coventry at a very early period ; the roads from the surrounding villages, in every direction, were literally crowded with human beings, particularly from the districts of Nuneaton, Bedworth, Foleshill, &c., and the town presented in appearance of unusual bustle, thousands of strangers arriving to witness this awful ceremony, and long before the hour appointed every spot were the least glimpse of the engine of death could be obtained, were one mass of living creatures ; we may say seldom was the town more crowded. Since last Saturday the wretched woman seems much to feel the unfortunate situation in which she has placed herself ; her conduct has quite corresponded with her awful situation, she continually talks about her child, and seems very anxious as to its future circumstances in life.

On Sunday night the culprit was very restless ; on Sunday slept most of the night ; and since that time she has been again restless, frequently calling upon God to have mercy on her soul.

The scaffold was erected in the front of the gaol, affording a commanding view from the church yard and neighbourhood, which being an extensive open space afforded little difficulty for viewing the awful ceremony ; and as usual a fair sprinkling of females were present. The under Sheriff arrived about the stated time to demand the culprit ; who at the time was deeply engaged in prayer. After the usual formalities, her arms were pinioned and the procession slowly moved forward, when the crowd manifested the greatest anxiety to obtain an early glance of the unfortunate criminal. She was respectably attired, and appeared deeply impressed with her awful situation ; but the moment she appeared, a death like silence seemed to prevail throughout the multitude assembled, followed by a mournful murmur from some of the by-standers. She appeared rather more pale than usual.

The executioner having placed the unfortunate woman under the fatal beam, proceeded to fix the cap and adjust the rope. All now being completed the signal was given and the unhappy culprit launched into eternity. After hanging the usual time, the body was removed back to the gaol for interment into the interior.

Mary Ball's Death Mask

As was common at the time for the famous or notorious recently deceased, a death mask was taken of Mary's face immediately following her death. We have no need for death masks now because we can use photographs for identification purposes.

The mask of Mary Ball may have been used for scientific purposes; it was common in the 1800s for scientists studying physiognomy to look for physical characteristics, especially of the face, to try and point out characteristics of criminals.

Thanks to the University of Warwick, with the use of the latest 3D scanning technology we have been able to laser scan and 3D print a copy of the original death mask (left), which has been in the Coventry Police Museum for many years. This means a copy of the mask can easily be displayed whilst the original is properly looked after and cared for.

The blue image below shows the high quality scan which is so detailed it even shows surface details such as wrinkles.

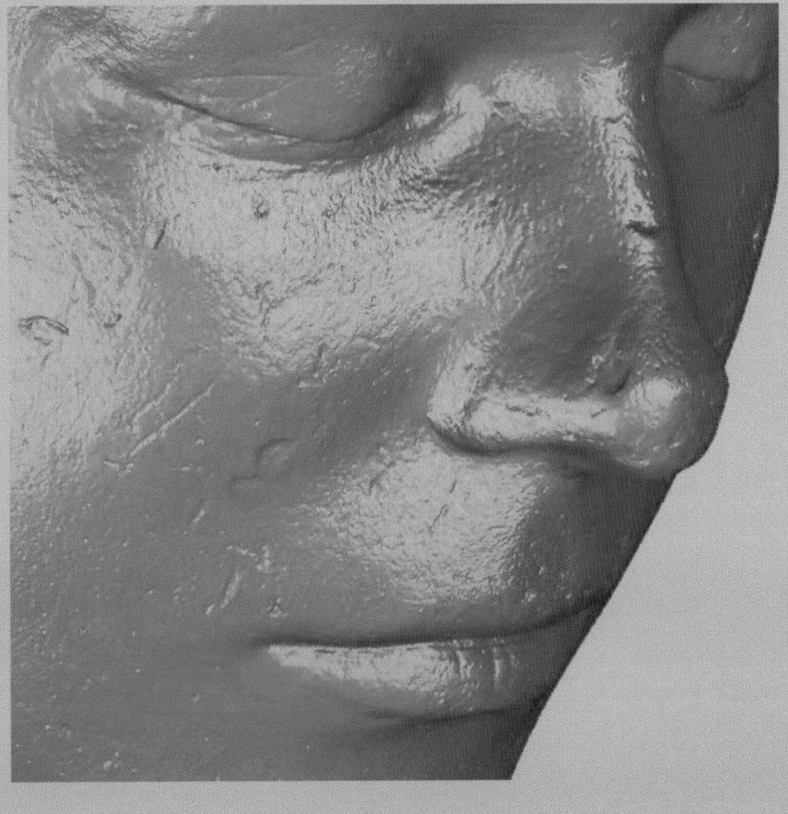

1939 IRA Bombing

On 25 August 1939, an Irish Republican Army bomb exploded in Coventry City Centre. This was part of the IRA's 'S' campaign, where they targeted British cities in an attempt to persuade Britain to withdraw from Northern Ireland and create an independent, united Ireland. The attack took place nine days before the outbreak of World War Two. A 5lb bomb was attached with a timer to a bicycle. When the bomb exploded five people died and 70 were injured. The bomb caused significant damage and Broadgate in Coventry City Centre resembled 'a miniature battlefield'

The aftermath of the explosion

The victims were:

Elsie Ansell, she was 21 years old, worked as a shop assistant nearby and was about to get married. She crossed the road to look at jewellery in a shop window when the bomb went off. She died instantly.

John Corbett Arnott, 15 years old, and **Rex Gentle** both worked at W H Smiths nearby in Hertford Street. Rex was sent to Coventry from Wales to provide holiday cover. He was lodging with John and had adjusted their breaks so they could have lunch together. They were returning from their lunch when the bomb went off.

Gwilym Rowland, a road sweeper, he was working on the pavement outside at the time the bomb exploded.

James Clay, a well know business man in Coventry, was a former president of the Coventry and District Co-Operative Society. He had been having lunch with a friend at a nearby cafe but had left earlier than usual, saying he felt unwell.

Many of the injured were left with long term damage from shrapnel[13].

Two men: Peter Barnes and James McCormick (under the name James Richards) - both from County Offaly, Ireland, were convicted for the bombing and sentenced to death. During his trial in Birmingham, McCormick insisted his orders were "not to endanger life". The two men were sentenced to death and were hung in Birmingham. This caused outrage in Ireland - the punishment of death was seen as too harsh, as the two men had not made or planted the bomb.

Another man Joby O'Sullivan was involved but was never caught. He was interviewed years later and was insistent that the placement of the bomb was accidental. He commented "The intention was to bomb the police station but the bicycle wheels kept getting stuck in the tram tracks" so he abandoned it and took off.[14]

After the bombing there was a strong anti-Irish feeling in Coventry; Irish men in lodgings were asked to find alternative accommodation and factory owners were threatened with strikes if they did not stop using Irish labour. Even Coventry's Chief Constable had to issue a statement to say he was not Irish: "I am a perfectly good Somerset man" he commented.[15]

A memorial stone for the victims of the attack was unveiled on 14 October 2015, it is located on Unity Lawn in the grounds of the cathedral.

Coventry Prisoners

The first image has been shared with the kind permission of Coventry Archives and shows the youngest prisoner in their book of mugshots in 1898: Oliver Hickman was around 17 years of age when arrested with Sidney John Jackson, both charged with stealing a canvas bag and a quantity of bones from outside a butchers, which they promptly sold on. One individual paid 1s 4d for eight pounds of bones from the boys! It was reported that Hickman had just completed his license period for a previous custodial sentence of five years in a reformatory, and was sent to prison for 28 days for this offence.

---

[13] https://www.historiccoventry.co.uk/articles/content.php?pg=not-forgotten
[14] https://www.bbc.co.uk/news/uk-england-coventry-warwickshire-28191501
[15] https://www.bbc.co.uk/news/uk-england-coventry-warwickshire-28191501

The below prisoner images have been kindly shared by Ian Wright and were the property of his grandfather Albert Edward Wright, likely used to help him identify the prolific or wanted criminals of the day:

Below left: Edward Thomas Jones – 'strongly suspected of committing offences in this city with John Hardy who is staying with him' in February of 1929. Below right: William Osmond Randle – house and shop breaker.

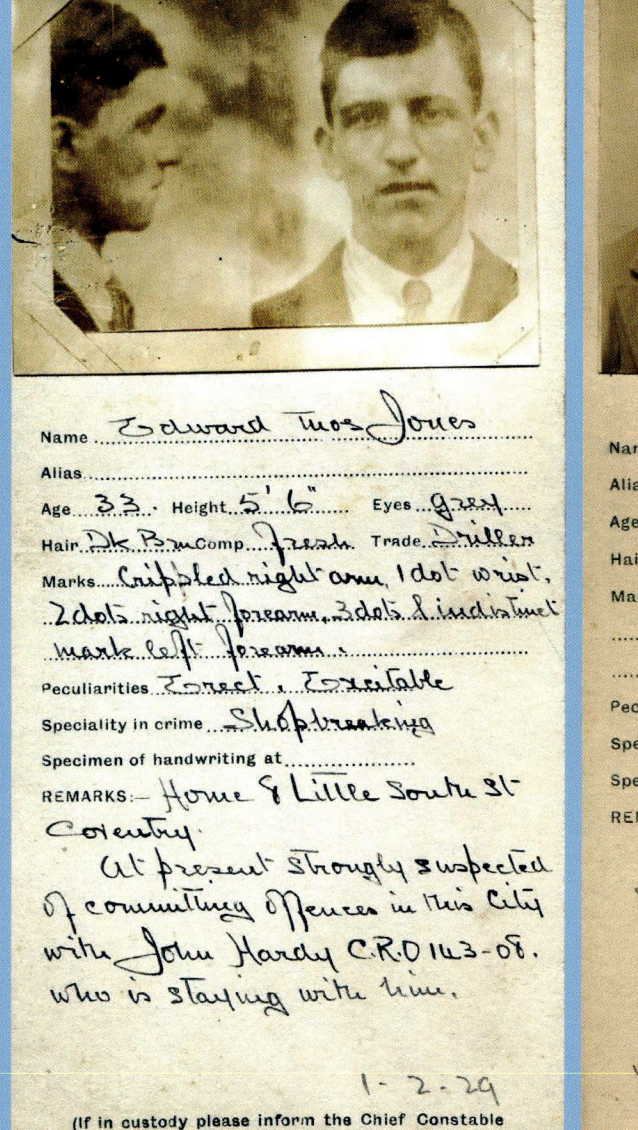
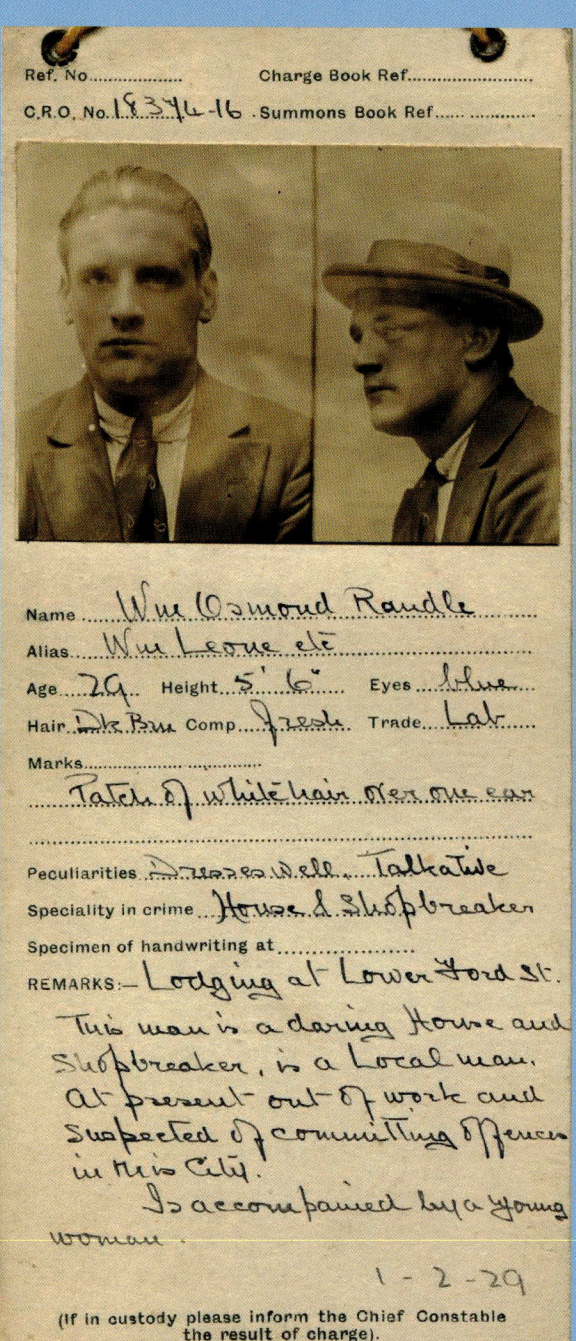

COVENTRY CITY POLICE.

Tele 4071-2-3.   ref D.O. 1256.   13th July 1930.

Wanted on Warrant in this City for Causing Grevious Bodily
Harm to P.C.Bettany, 135, on the 5th inst.

C.E.McCALLASKEY, @ WARD, known as Jerry.

Age 21 years, 5'7", good build,
Auburn hair, with sideboards,
fresh comp, clean shaven,
eyes slightly crossed.
Wearing, Cap, brown suit, or
Plum coloured jacket, and
dirty grey flannel trousers.
Irish Nationality.

DANIEL GARRITY, known as DANNY.

Age 20 years, 5'9"-10", good build,
light hair, with sideboards,
clean shaven, fresh comp,
Wearing, Check cap,
Blue suit,
Scotch Nationality.

The above named are of the labouring class, and may be found on
buildings in course of erection.

Please cause enquiries to be made and any information obtained
please communicate with the undersigned.

City Police Office   S.A.Hector.

Above – wanted on warrant for causing grievous bodily harm to PC Bettany: C. E. McAllaskey & Daniel Garrity, 13 July 1930

7. World War I

In August 1914, the strength of Coventry City Police was 137. When the country's 'call for service' came, a large number of those volunteered to fight. It was important that sufficient men were kept at home to help keep Coventry safe, so with the introduction of the special constabulary – the Chief Constable was able to spare 50 men.

Some Coventry policemen were decorated whilst overseas – like Constable King (later sergeant) who served with the force from 1907 to 1934. In 1917 he wrote back home to say that he was very surprised to receive the Military Medal, because he did not know what he had done to deserve it, other than carrying out some very awkward jobs.

It was stated in the Coventry Standard 19 January 1917 that Constable King MM was the first member of the force to be decorated. The article went on to say Constable King was serving with the 'Coventry Fortress Company, now a company of the Royal Engineers' and held the rank of sergeant.

At least two other members of the force also received the Military Medal – including Cyril George Boneham (whose story is covered later) and Bombardier E C Porter.

Of the 50 men who left for the Armed Forces, 10 did not return:

PC Abraham Lucas. Lance Corporal 7084. 1st Battalion Liecestershire Regiment. Died in Belgium 5 February 1915.

Abraham joined the police in December 1911, after serving in the Army in Madras, India. At the outbreak of war he re-joined the Army and promptly achieved promotion to Lance Corporal.

He died of his wounds aged 28 and is commemorated at Ploegsteert Memorial in Hainaut, Belgium. Cemetery/memorial reference: Panel 4.

PC Charles Edwin Gabbitas. Lance Corporal 15937. 11th Battalion Royal Warwickshire Regiment. Died in England 26 August 1916 aged 22.

Charles was mortally wounded by shell fire at a base camp and died following evacuation to the UK. He is buried in South Muskham (St Wilfrid) Churchyard in Nottinghamshire. The footnote on his headstone reads *Now sleeps the brave who sinks to rest, by all his country's wishes blest*.

PC Thomas Jennings. Corporal 6414 Machine Gun Corps

Died in France 15 September 1916.

Thomas was killed in action on 15 September 1916, aged 30. He is commemorated on the Thiepval Memorial, Somme, France.

Cemetery/memorial reference: Pier and Face 5 C and 12 C.

PC Oliver Jephcott Randle. Lance Corporal 16635

10 Battalion Royal Warwickshire Regiment. Died in France 18 November 1916.

Oliver chose to follow in his father's footsteps and became a police constable in the Coventry City Police. Shortly after the outbreak of war he enlisted in the Royal Warwickshire Regiment.

He was killed in action at the battle of the Grandecourt on 18 November 1916, aged 26.

PC Charles Davis Brown. Private 12011 1st Battalion Grenadier Guards. Died in France 9 December 1916

Charles' father was also a police constable, with the Metropolitan Police Service.

In the 1911 census Charles' occupation is shown as a constable in the Coventry City Police.

He died of his wounds on 9 December 1916, aged 29.

PC Frank Webb, Serjeant 12757 11 Battalion Royal Warwickshire Regiment. Died in France 26 April 1917

Frank was one of two sons of Thomas and Jane Webb, who resided in Hearsall Common, Canley Gates, Coventry.

He died of his wounds on 26 April 1917, aged 29. Frank is buried at Duisans British Cemetery, Etrun, France in Pas de Calais, France. Cemetery/memorial reference: IV. H. 5.

PC Albert Edward Smith. Serjeant 12736 of the 15th Battalion (2nd Birmingham Pals) Royal Warwickshire Regiment. Died in Belgium 26 October 1917

Albert was a member of the Coventry City Police and enlisted in the Royal Warwickshire Regiment in Coventry.

He was killed in action on 26 October 1917, aged 30. Albert is commemorated at Tyne Cot Memorial in West-Vlaanderen, Belgium. Memorial reference: Panel 23 to 28

PC John James. Serjeant 266468 of the 2/5 Battalion Royal Warwickshire Regiment.

Died in France 3 December 1917.

John died aged 23 and is commemorated at Cambrai Memorial, Louveral, in Nord, France. The number of casualties recorded is 7,118. Cemetery/memorial reference: Panel 3.
FAG Memorial ID: 56027596

PC George Kings. Serjeant 33104 of the 1st battalion Duke of Edinburgh's Regiment

Died in France 27 May 1918.

George was a member of the Coventry City Police and enlisted for the 1st Battalion, Duke of Edinburgh's (Wiltshire) Regiment in Coventry.
George died of his wounds on 27 May 1918, aged 29. He is commemorated on the Soissons Memorial. France

PC Joseph Arthur Richards. Captain of the 8th Battalion Royal Warwickshire regiment.

Died in France 4 November 1918

His death was reported in the paper as: *'Acting captain in the 8th Royal Warwickshire Regiment died 4th November 1918 at Landrecies, France in action.'* There were reported to be 151 casualties. Joseph was only 26 years of age. He is buried at Landrecies British Cemetery, Nord, France – memorial reference A. 31. He is also commemorated at St Cuthberts' Church, Shustoke on their Roll of Honour and a tree was planted in his memory.

The picture over the following page shows Coventry City policemen at the train station on their way to join the Armed Forces. Future Chief Constable William Imber stands behind them on the right page:

8. Coventry Bobbies

We are fortunate to have received pictures and information within the museum to tell the stories of a handful of Coventry bobbies throughout the 1900s.

Thomas Golby

Thomas Golby joined Coventry City Police in 1868 and stories passed down through his family indicate he was the first Coventry City Police officer to travel overseas to make an arrest – going all the way to Melboune, Australia to arrest a lawyer who had absconded with money from clients. Thomas retired in the rank of inspector in 1894.

Walter Bowers

Thanks to Walter's grandson Geoff for pictures and information relating to his grandfather. Walter Bowers was born in Lincolnshire in 1884 and served in the Army for eight years before joining Coventry City Police in 1910. He was commended during his first year for detecting a fire. Upon the outbreak of war in 1914 he joined the Military Police, returning to the Coventry police in 1919. By 1920 he was transferred to the Criminal Investigation Department and in 1921 he was given a monetary reward for his work in connection with a house-breaker who had twice escaped from Dartmoor Prison and subsequently Winson Green. The man had stolen a loaded revolver and it was Walter's work that led to his arrest.

He was back in uniform in 1922 upon promotion to patrol sergeant, subsequently being promoted to patrol inspector four years later, before returning to the CID in 1932 as Chief Inspector Bowers, where he took charge of the department for the next seven years. Chief Inspector Bowers retired on superannuation in 1939, handing the reigns over to Chief Inspector Cyril Boneham.

Walter is seated on the right, pictured with his CID colleagues

Below: Walter (seated second from the right) with CID colleagues including a young DC Pendleton – far left seated

We are unsure of the occasion, but this picture likely shows the vast majority of the Coventry City Police, c1920s. *With thanks to Ian Wright.*

Albert Edward Wright

Thanks to Ian Wright for the information and photographs relating to his grandfather Albert Edward Wright, most of which have featured throughout this booklet Albert was born in 1890 in Countesthorpe and joined the Coventry City Police on 10 January 1912, being posted to the Central Division. His records show that in May 1915 he left the police to join the Armed Forces, serving in the Royal Warwickshire Regiment, 13th Battalion. Albert returned to Coventry in April 1919 and wasted no time getting straight back to business – being commended for prompt action at a fire in November that year. As with many police officers at the time, he took a keen interest in sports, playing in the cricket and football teams (in the cricket picture on page 50, Albert is seen sat in front of Chief Constable William Imber).

In June 1922 Albert was commended again and given a £2 gratuity for alertness and tact in connection with the apprehension of cycle thieves. By October 1922 Albert had been transferred to the Detectives Department, but returned to uniform upon promotion to sergeant in May 1923. Albert was to be commended two more times – once in March 1929 for a case of loitering with intent and once in June 1939 in connection with explosions cases, two months before the fatal bombing on Broadgate that killed five people.

During the Second World War, Albert was injured when the police station at St Mary Street suffered a direct hit, killing several of his colleagues.

He retired in 1945, after completing 33 years' service.

Thomas Wilson

Thomas Wilson was born in 1899 in Nuneaton. Prior to joining the police, he served for 13 months as a private in the Shropshire Light Infantry. When he joined Coventry City Police as PC 1 in May 1923, his previous occupation was recorded as tailor.

He moved satisfactorily through the ranks and was first commended by the Watch Committee in 1927 for stopping a runaway horse, and again in 1939 for arresting a shop-breaker. Thomas was one of several officers who closely policed Winston Churchill's famous visit to Coventry after the conclusion of World War II and he can be identified in the Churchill pic on page 65 by the number one on his collar.

We have been sent another wonderful picture of Thomas by his granddaughter Helen, of him on traffic points duty (where officers would direct traffic at busy interchanges, many of which are now controlled by traffic lights) looking a bit bemused as a performer cycles past him.

With thanks to Helen Hart for the photographs

Fred Withers GM

PC Fred Withers GM joined Coventry City Police following service with the Royal Air Force from 1941 to 1946, when he was awarded the George Medal along with two colleagues for the rescue of a soldier who was severely injured when the other three officers in his unit were killed. To do this, they had to wade through a canal, go through a barbed wire fence and cross a minefield to retrieve the soldier before placing him on a stretcher and bringing him to safety. It was stated in the citation that they showed great fortitude and initiative, and complete disregard for their own safety.

January 1948, Fred had a brief break in service from January 1949, before re-joining 14 October 1952. He was commended for an arrest for shop-breaking in 1948, and after re-joining the force rose through the ranks to Chief Inspector, serving as part of Warwickshire & Coventry Constabulary and also West Midlands Police before retiring in September 1975. During his service he was one of many officers around the country that delivered mutual aid in Aberfan after the disaster there in 1966 that saw the collapse of a colliery spoil tip which killed 144 people, many of them schoolchildren.

Fred and colleague with signals van in Aberfan

Fred working as the sergeant in the Control Room c1960s.

Fred's son Bob (along with many other people no doubt) used to listen in to the police network when his father worked in the Information Room, listening out for his father's voice. He recalls one story where an unfortunate PC clipped the kerb on the A45 and damaged the suspension on a Triumph Vitesse traffic car. Fred's reassuring advice was to 'limp back to the yard and I'll try and get Cyril Warner [the mechanic] to meet you there before the end of your shift', much to the PC's relief!

With thanks to Fred's son Bob and daughter Janice for the pictures and information.

9. Coventry City Police's Female Officers

The topic of women police first appears in the Watch Committee minutes in Coventry in 1919. Due to the success of the Voluntary Women's Patrols in the area, the secretary of the Coventry branch of the National Council of Women asked if the appointment of women police was being considered as 'social workers in the city felt strongly that the presence of fully trained and qualified women police would be of great benefit to the wellbeing of the citizens'. The Watch Committee however, had no intention of considering any such thing.[16]

Once in 1924 and twice during 1934 the question of women police was again brought to the Watch Committee but they would not reverse their decision – despite the issuance of Home Office regulations on the conditions of employment and two Government Commissions recommending an increase in numbers of policewomen.

In 1935 the Watch Committee held a vote on a recommendation that women police would NOT be appointed with 23 to 19 voting in favour of them not being appointed. It would be another three years before Coventry would appoint its first female police officers.

Following increased pressure from the Home Office, minutes from the Watch Committee in September 1937 show that they were starting to consider how women police could be usefully employed, particularly in dealing with women, girls and juvenile offenders. The success of women matrons in dealing with female prisoners is mentioned and a recommendation was passed for two women constables to be appointed in April 1938, subject to approval from the Secretary of State.[17]

This was approved and on 25 April 1938 two female officers were recruited – Ena Goodacre and Kathleen Rowe. In their report to the Watch Committee in November 1939,[18] they outline the work they have carried out so far. This starts with their training at the Birmingham Police Training School which included the standard training for male recruits, but also additional training with the Women Police and the lady enquiry officers based within the Birmingham CID. They learned how to take statements and received advice in how to interview women and girls regarding sexual offences.

After completion of their training in July 1938 they returned to Coventry and during their first year:

- Interviewed 1,048 women and girls
- Took 277 statements
- Acted as escort to 53 women and girls
- Made 32 arrests

The women highlight that much of their work related to parents asking them for advice, claiming their daughters were out of control and they didn't know what to do. A lot of referrals were also made to the policewomen in relation to girls and women in need of help, lodgings and/or employment. This is very similar to the early years of the Birmingham City Women Police where their work consisted mainly of assisting with social welfare issues.

The women state that the escort duties they carried out included taking women and girls to various hostels, remand homes and prisons. Interestingly they include the Birmingham Police Women's Hostel

---

[16] Forty Years of Women's Work, 1917-1957, PA1269/7/1 – courtesy of the Herbert Art Gallery
[17] Coventry City Watch Committee Minutes, Sept 28 1937, p1361
[18] Report of the Police Women to the Coventry City Watch Committee – 14 November 1939, courtesy of Herbert Art Gallery

(which would have been Newton Street by this time) as one of the recipients of the women they assisted.

The report goes on to say:

> 'The arrests have chiefly been for shop-lifting, although there have been a number of girls arrested and charged with being in need of care and protection, or in moral danger.
>
> For the first three months of our work here, there was some reluctance on the part of the public to bring matters to our notice. This has considerably altered. Whereas in the first three months of our work we interviewed 146 women and girls, in the last three months we have interviewed 252.
>
> In addition to our work in connection with women and girls, we have spent considerable lengthy periods in observation work on I.R.A. activities, indecency complaints, and on periodical complaints of thefts from the person.
>
> During the first few months of our work, we spent considerable periods patrolling public parks and commons, and also visited the various Women's lavatories, with a certain amount of success, but owing to the above observations which took up some of our time, we had to somewhat curtail these, but we hope in the near future to give more attention to this.'

Ena Goodacre

Ena was born in 1911 and spent her early years on her family's farm. She had an interest in rifles from an early age and used to practise target shooting with an air rifle. After joining Coventry City Police in 1938, she became the force's first female sergeant in December 1943.

After the war she joined the Probation Service and in 1957 moved to Vancouver, Canada, where she picked up another accolade – British Colombia's first female probation officer. She returned to England in 1963, continuing to work in the Probation Service until she retired in 1976. She joined a local shooting club and won many trophies. She was also part of a British shooting team sent to Canada in 1974. In 1988 she again made history by being the National Rifle Association's Captain of the British ladies team sent to compete against Australia. This was the first and only time the British NRA sent a women's fullbore rifle team to any overseas championships. Ena was very much respected for her wisdom and calming influence, as well as her non-judgmental insight into people and events. She never married and died on February 24 2008[19].

Ena Goodacre - Coventry Evening Telegraph, 16 December 1943

---

[19] Obituary of Ena Goodacre, which appeared in The Times March 17 2008 and the NRA Journal Summer 2008

Kathleen Rowe

Kathleen was 27 when she joined Coventry Police alongside Ena – going straight into the CID. She stated in an interview in My Weekly from June 1 1996, that her cousin's husband encouraged her to join after seeing an article in The Police Review which said that more women were being recruited. She originally applied for the Metropolitan Police but was turned down. Their loss was Coventry's gain!

She stated she never felt opposition from her male counterparts, but felt they were always very supportive. Kathleen recalls the investigation into the 1939 IRA bombing campaign and how she spoke a lot to a female prisoner, eventually being able to convince her to give the evidence needed bring the bombers to trial.

Kathleen also recalled on other occasions where male officers were protective of her and if things got a bit heated, asked her to retreat to safety and protected her from foul language. She stated that male colleagues (and criminals!) always showed her the utmost of respect. Unlike todays policewomen dealing with riots, assaults and other dangerous situations - Kathleen stated that the most confrontation female officers had back then, was being asked to deal with drunken women!

She also recalled some difficult times during the Coventry Blitz having to respond to queries from relatives asking if their family members were ok after bombing raids and trying to prevent looting. Unfortunately Police Regulations at the time meant that Kathleen was forced to retire upon her marriage four years into her service as Coventry had not relaxed the 'marriage ban' for policewomen, which several other forces had done during the War. She went on to have three children and we are thankful to Wendy and Anne for sharing details of their mother's service.

They recall she was a natural detective and transitioned perfectly into a role as a store detective after she left the police. They also remember how she would 'police' a war memorial in the city, ensuring children treated it with respect and didn't play on it. Kathleen met her husband during World War 2 when he was fire watching on the roof of the Coventry Council House – presumably narrowly missing the bomb that landed on the police station!

Margery Whittaker

Margery Whittaker is believed to be the first former policewoman in the West Midlands area to reach 100 years of age, back in 2018. She joined Coventry City Police in 1940 and would have therefore been one of the earliest policewomen in the city, marrying fellow officer Gerry Whittaker, later Chief Superintendent of A Division at Little Park Street Police Station.

Margery Whittaker

Mary Gallagher (nee Weir)

We were lucky enough to discover Mary Gallagher's story when her daughter Patricia approached us to help commemorate her mother turning 100 years of age on 8 February 2021. Patricia spoke to her mother to find out more details of her police service for us to add to our archives. The following are from Mary's recollections:

'The Second World War ended in 1945 and I joined in the Coventry City Police in 1946. As I joined police women only worked in their plain clothes. Soon afterwards I returned to Coventry from training school in Ryton on Dunsmore. Chief Constable Edward Pendleton was a local Coventry man and had been to Bablake Grammar School, worked his way up the Force and was appointed Chief. By then, during the previous Chief's time, we had been transferred to wearing uniform. One of the women wouldn't wear uniform so she left. I remained on the Force ten years: leaving in 1956 – now married.

As policewomen we were paid a little less than policemen and it was necessary to work for two years on probation before you were accepted as a full police officer, which I did. We were treated the same as the men. We did not [wear] handcuffs but we had the same powers of arrest in every other way as the men. We did a variety of jobs as they came along, as did the men. We had the power of arrest for any offence that we were aware of because we had full training and knowledge of police law. I found it very interesting as I like the mixing with people. Our job – the actual motto was 'Protection of Life and Property'. That was what we were there for and in my case I found it very interesting, very satisfying work – it suited me down to the ground.

We worked the same system of shifts as did the men. I never heard any adverse reports about women police and I found the attitude of the public very pleasant indeed. We never knew what was around the corner – what was going to happen – but whatever happened had to be dealt with.

We experienced regularly reports of women shoppers in the market having their purses stolen. One day I was on duty in the market in uniform on a Saturday and I noticed a fellow trying to steal a purse and for some reason the woman moved so he didn't get it, but he moved away so I moved as well, followed him. He left the market straight away so I deduced that he would only leave the market if he had got something, so I stopped him and I told him why I was arresting him and I cautioned him. And I wanted what was in his pocket which he said it was a gun. I said, "Alright, give me the gun." Because his hand was still in his pocket, I moved swiftly aside in case his pocket went bang! I persisted of course, he was under arrest then, so he eventually gave up this purse. He wasn't very nice. He gave it up and I put it in my pocket. I got a message to the police office – you see at that time we didn't carry telephones – no means of getting directly in touch if we'd made an arrest. But I managed with some help from a member of the public to get in touch with the office to ask for a car. This was in Smithford Street, Coventry, but I did not risk walking with him under arrest to Broadgate because there were crowds of people and this fellow might easily have tried to mingle with the crowd and ask for help and some person could have easily helped him to get from my grasp. So we stood still until the police got the message and sent a car. We get to the office and of course, we had had so many thefts, that the fact someone had been arrested raised eyebrows with delight. The detective superintendent came into the charge office where this fellow was with me and the sergeant and he was very interested to see this man because he said when he was a young policeman this same fellow came in as a prisoner and was put in the cell. The prisoner rang the bell, the PC was sent to him and he asked for a drink of water. This it appears, is an old trick, so the PC took a cup of water and he [the prisoner] promptly threw the water over the PC. Once when I had a woman prisoner in the cell, she asked for water and she was about to throw it over me, when I put my hands on my hips in a menacing manner and said, "Alright, go on!" and she didn't throw the water ... she drank it. However, this detective superintendent recognised this fellow. He was a man, I believe, of 74 years and he had spent over 40 years in prisons up and down the country for all kinds of events, including ten years for attempted murder, ten years for grievous bodily harm and various lengths in prisons for all kinds of offences: house-breaking, thefts, assaults, anything you could think of in police law – he had done it.

The man was sent to prison for seven years, Mary was commended for the manner in which she gave her evidence, and during the next government inspection of Coventry City Police, the case was brought up and she had to relay all the circumstances to the whole force, who were assembled for inspection!

Mary in 2021

Myrtle Jesperson (left) is another policewoman from the 1950s. She served in the early 1950s at Parkside (pic courtesy of Jo Soanes) and was also the sister of Inspector Bob Jespersen.

Pictured below are some female officers with Assistant Inspector of Constabulary Jean Law (a former Birmingham City policewoman) around 1976. Left to right: Joan Jones, Janice Wade and Rose Cole, along with Jean Law.

By January 1957 an Inspector, Mrs Joanne Green, is referenced as outlining the history of the women's branch to the Watch Committee and in November 1957 she was showing visitors round the new force headquarters. Inspector Green initially spent two years with Kent County Constabulary from 1944 to 1946 and the following ten years with Rochdale Borough Police before joining Coventry City Police in June 1956. She may have been the first female inspector in Coventry.

Sergeant Brenda Ward was the first female officer to complete 22 years' service in Coventry – she received her long service medal here from Warwickshire and Coventry Chief Constable Richard Matthews on 8 August 1973. She retired in 1976 after completing 25 years' service.

10. Sport and Recreation

As with other police forces around the country, sport played a big part of the life of officers from Coventry City Police. Pictures of some of the different teams are shown below:

The below pictures are from Ian Wright and contain his grandfather Albert Edward Wright (central in white jumper in first picture and seated left in cricket team). The above picture is from the museum but also appears to show Albert in the goalie jumper:

Above: Cricket Team c1920 and below: Tug of War Team c1912. Sgt James Johnson standing second from right (pic courtesy of Malcolm Parker)

Coventry City Police Bible Class 1891

Religion was a big part of many officer's lives in the 1800s and early 1900s, similar to the rest of society. This picture shows the Bible Class of 1891.

11. World War II

Britain had already been preparing for war well before it began in September 1939. Like other major cities and towns, Coventry had already started preparations to protect its residents from air raids. The population had been issued with gas mask ahead of anticipated gas attacks and preparations made for residents to have access to air raid shelters. Some were fortunate to have their own Anderson shelters for the gardens, other had Morrison shelters insider their houses but most shelters were communal. Originally just trenches in parks, they soon proved inadequate and were concrete lined to keep out the elements and provide better protection. Like many other cities Coventry would receive attention from the Luftwaffe, the German air force who legitimised the attacks as the factories of Coventry were heavily involved in the production of war material, particularly aircraft production. There were a total of 41 enemy raids over Coventry but two in particular would forever change the look of Coventry as the Luftwaffe attempted to burn the heart out of the city.

The defence of the city was to use a modern phrase, a 'multi-agency approach'. The military controlled anti-aircraft guns (the 3.7 calibre gun could hurl a 13lb shell to 35,000 feet into the air), and then there was a more passive defence in the form of barrage balloons which could reach a height of 8,000 feet. Designed to discourage enemy aircraft not wishing to collide with the steel cables holding them, they forced planes to fly higher with the resultant effect of reducing bombing accuracy. Sadly they were to prove just as dangerous to British aircraft which strayed too close.

These measures though did not prevent heavy bombing, and on the ground it was the police who had responsibility for co-ordinating the response to these attacks. Just a stone's throw from the cathedral in St Mary Street stood the police station. From the control room in the basement the police responded to and controlled incidents; co-ordinating the other services such as ambulance, other medical services, fire, wardens and military personnel.

Picture of the police control room in St Mary Street Police Station during war time. Note the sign saying 'Casualty Control' – courtesy of David McGrory

Similar to other forces up and down the country, Coventry lost many of its officers to service with the Armed Forces during World War II, and additional people were needed to carry out the vital work policing the city. To fill those gaps the police employed the following:

- Considerably more special constables (unpaid police officers) who often left to join the Armed Forces themselves
- Police War Reserve Constables (PWRC) individuals recruited specifically during wartime on a different contract to a regular constable, but carrying out very similar work. Many individuals became war reserve constables as an option for their National Service as opposed to joining the Armed Forces.
- Women's Auxiliary Police Corps (WAPC) a team of highly trained, drilled and disciplined women who carried out a variety of administrative roles to support the force – such as manning the front desk, dealing with enquiries into absent soldiers and helping to deal with the co-ordination of emergency services following air raids.
- Police Auxiliary Messenger Service (PAMS) were boys aged 16-18, keen to do their bit for the war effort but too young for the Armed Forces or to become special constables. They played a vital role taking messengers between stations, to officers or other emergency services, often whilst air raids were taking place.

In total 14 officers were to be killed due to enemy action and sadly two members of the PAMS also perished. The youngest of these was Thomas Lowry aged just 16.

On the 14 November 1940 one of the largest and most devastating raids took place. At 18:17 Kampfgruppe 100 pathfinders consisting of 13 Heinkel 111s, droned across Lyme Bay Dorset carrying 10,224 incendiary and 48 x 100lb bombs heading for Coventry. At 19:05 the first indication of an impending air raid was given when the 'yellow' warning was given, meaning that invaders had been detected. This was followed a few minutes later by the second warning, purple, meaning invaders were expected to pass over the area. Hopes that the Luftwaffe were just passing had gone by 19:10 when the red warning was given and by 19:24 the first bombs had fallen. Any initial thoughts that this raid would soon pass were dispelled as further waves of enemy aircraft appeared above the city to rain death and destruction down on its inhabitants.

Example of a 1kg incendiary bomb next to an 18 inch ruler.

It was on this night that Coventry Cathedral was destroyed. Coventry historian David McGrory covers the bombing of Coventry Cathedral in his book Coventry Blitz, which much of the below information is from.

At seven o'clock the Provost of Coventry, the very Revd R T Howard, met his fire watchers on the roof of the nave of St Michael. Within five minutes of the siren sounding the bombers could be heard over the city and fires began to take hold. By 19:40 the first incendiary hit the cathedral. This was the first of many the brave men tackled throughout the raid. It was reported that at one point a police officer and soldier had climbed up onto the roof and entered into their own private battle throwing incendiaries of the battlements. After a while the policeman had to leave after an incendiary exploded and blasted phosphorus into his face. The fight to save the cathedral was lost and like most of the inner city, lay in ruins.

During this horrendous raid several Coventry Police officers lost their lives, valiantly attempting to save other people.

King George VI at Coventry's ruined cathedral, 16 November 1940, from a painting by Frederick Roe held in the Police Museum in Coventry – note Chief Constable Stanley Hector to the left

The below account was written by PC 76 Wilfred Lambert who had joined Coventry City Police in May 1939. Parts of it were written shortly after arriving home following completion of his shift during the devastating air raid on the 14th November 1940. This makes his words even more powerful, as his memory would have been crystal clear of the horrors he had just witnessed. The air raids that night had left 568 dead and 863 severely injured[20]. His sister Olive told us how he sat down at the table and started to write:

"Today had been a lovely Autumn day and I had been for a swim – little knowing that it would be my last for weeks to come, and within a few hours the baths would be a heap of rubble.

At this time my mother and sisters had been going out to Berkswell to sleep owing to previous severe raids on Coventry. On this particular day I rode to the Central Police Station ready to answer the sirens which had sounded just after blackout time for weeks past.

Twilight had fallen by this time and we could see it was going to be a perfect night for a raid. Streets were full of people and shops were all displaying a plentiful supply of goods. Broadgate, Smithford Street, Cross Cheaping, Hertford Street, and in fact all the town looked just as it had done for years, yet, by tomorrow all this would be one mess of blazing rubble and a scene of desolation. As I entered the station door the Cathedral was towering majestically at the end of the street, although the priceless glass-stained windows had been removed soon after the outbreak of war. The moon was well in the heavens and was perfectly round.

At five past seven the 'RED' alert came through and the sirens sounded their warnings. By this time most people were in shelters, as was their usual custom for the night, and the people who went out to sleep at night had left the City in one long trail of their motor cars.

Within five minutes of the warning the drone of the Luftwaffe could be heard overhead, and incendiary bombs had been dropped in a shower over the city. By 7.15pm the men who were usually at the Station in readiness for the sirens to sound, had been lined up in the corridor. The first incident to be reported to the Central Control was a public shelter believed to have been hit in Warwick Road and a number of

---

[20] Coventry Blitz by David McGrory

people trapped. P.C. Bill Timms No.82 and I, and two Specials were sent out to the occurrence. When we stepped out of the Station, even after 15 minutes we could see it was going to be a heavy raid, but how heavy we never dreamed. The air was filled with the crash of guns, the whine of bombs and the terrific flash and bang as they exploded. The sky seemed to be full of planes, and indeed it was before the raid was over, for 500 took part in it – both German and Italian.

We made our way along high Street and down Greyfriars Lane and as we passed the Midland Bank we could see the roof was blazing furiously and firemen were trying to get it under control. Before we reached Warwick Road we must have dropped flat a dozen times and thought our ends were near. However, the report turned out to be false and we began our journey back to the Station. We put several incendiaries out and as we passed Greyfriars Green a shower dropped here, and we had our first experience of the explosive type. As we rushed to extinguish one on the Green, it exploded, and blazing metal flew in all directions. A young A.F.S. (Auxiliary Fire Service) messenger and P.C. Timms were badly burned in the face and eyes. We took the messenger boy down Greyfriars Green shelter, rendered First Aid and rang for the ambulance.

The Ambulance seemed a long time coming, in fact it took three quarters of an hour to do about a mile, so heavy was the raid by this time.

Our party of four then started back to the Police Station. When we eventually reached Broadgate, the town seemed alight. Owen and Owen's new store was a blazing inferno and completely out of control, although firemen were still pouring water on it. Smithford Street and High Street were both ablaze, and some of the familiar old shops began to disappear in smoke and flame.

We eventually reached the Police Station at about 10.30pm and learned that during our absence, incendiaries had fallen on the Police Station roof but had been extinguished. Then a report was received saying that the Cathedral had caught fire and was beginning to get a hold. I went inside and saw that one corner of the roof was on fire. Firemen had arrived by this time and the hoses were connected up. We could see it would not be very hard to put out, but when the water was turned on, nothing happened. The water mains were fractured and no water was coming through! The hoses were later laid to the River Sherbourne in Priory Street, but it was too late to save the most famous building in Coventry. The roof collapsed within two hours and by morning there was nothing left but the spire and the four outside walls towering to the sky.

All this time bombs were falling, and when I went into the Police Station the doors were flying backwards and forwards by the terrific blast which was going through the building like a whirlwind. Most of the windows had been blown out and the blinds were flapping in the blast. Nearly all our telephones had been put out of action, so what few reports that came through, were delivered by hand. A message came to say that a shelter under Smith's, the Furnishers, in Jordan Well had been hit, and fourteen people were trapped underneath the debris in a cellar. A volunteer rescue party was formed and P.C. Rollins, Timms, four Specials, Inspector Ward and myself, went. I worked relief, and most of the digging was done by the P.C.'s. If ever two men deserved a medal, they did, but they did not even know their efforts were all in vain. They both took off their coats and were working in shirt sleeves, tunnelling under huge piles of debris, with spades and pick axes. The debris was passed back along a chain of rescuers, and dumped out of the way.

After about an hour, I was asked by P.C. Rollins to try and get some more help from the Police Station. I had just reached there, when Inspector Ward staggered along St. Mary Street and said that the rescue party at Smiths had all been killed by a direct hit. I went with him and saw all five of the rescue party lying on top of a heap of bricks and debris. They were all blackened and burned, but, recognisable. A rescue party was then despatched from the Police Station, but the five men were all beyond aid. This proved that a bomb can fall in the same place twice, contrary to all sayings. This bomb must have glanced off the only remaining wall of Smiths, so that the explosion occurred over the five men's heads, which explains why they were not blown to bits.

The heat from the surrounding fires by this time was terrific, and I had to keep knocking bits of burning material off my uniform. Brick-ends and rubble were flying through the air, and it was so light that one could see buildings collapsing right and left. The town was deserted by this time, and as I made my way up Gosford Street from the G.E.C. fire, it seemed like hell on Earth. One got so used to the scream of bombs that it was possible to tell almost to inches just where the bombs would explode, with a blinding and ear-splitting crash. Then would come the bomb blast that was so powerful at times, it took off doors and what few windows there were left.

I slowly made my way over heaps of debris and round bomb craters to the Police Station. It seemed almost laughable to be putting out incendiaries while the whole city burned. When I arrived at the Police Station, I could see the roof of the Cathedral had collapsed and shows of sparks and flames were coming from it. The Police Station was then surrounded by fire, every building along Jordan Well, Earl Street, Hay Lane, and Bayley Lane was ablaze. It was impossible to try and put out the fires, and all one could do was just sit or lay and wait to see how long it would be before a bomb hit us. Standing in St. Mary Street I saw several land mines floating down by parachute. They could easily be seen in the light of fires, and one or two actually exploded in mid-air, probably by the bullets which were being fired at them.

Coventry Cathedral in the aftermath of the bombing

At 6.15pm the 'WHITE' was received, but the sirens were unable to sound the 'ALL-clear', owing to there being no power to blow the sirens. At about 7.00am a few workers and spectators began to walk the streets, and what a sight it must have been for those who had spent the whole 11 hour raid down the shelters. It was indescribable. Fire engines and Ambulances were coming from the neighbouring towns, - some had been coming in during the raid and several fire-crews were wiped out even before they finished travelling.

When daylight came, a huge black pool of smoke hung over the city, and buildings were still collapsing right and left. I then met a Rescue and Ambulance Party from Birmingham in Smithford Street. I had to take them through fires and over debris until we reached Grosvenor Road, where we set about rescuing some people under a house which had received a direct hit by a H.E. (High Explosive bomb). We only fetched out one alive, the other three lay twisted and all covered by dust, and plaster, trapped by the ground floor which had trapped them in a cellar underneath when it had collapsed. I then walked back to the Police Station. As I came up Hertford Street, the heat from the fires was terrific. There were a few sightseers about by this time, but all roads leading to the City had been covered and only essential services were allowed in.

It was a pitiful sight at the Police Station when I arrived. People were collecting and asking for information. Some had lost their homes, others had missed their relations, everyone looked tired and weary, but no-one appeared to be worrying about sleep. I then went to Priory Street where there was an unexploded bomb in the road and remained on duty there until 2.30pm when I was relieved.

At 3pm a few of us were allowed to go home for a wash and a meal. We had been on our feet from the beginning of the raid until then and without a bite to eat. I cycled home as well as I could, in some parts I had to dismount and carry my cycle over debris. When I was passing the Morris works I saw a whole workshop blown into the air as a land-mine went off with a terrific explosion.

I reached home just after 3pm and found that a land mine had exploded three houses away from ours. Four or five houses were demolished. The roof was stripped off ours, the inside walls down, all doors and windows out, and the shed, garage, and all fences looked as if a tornado had hit them. I had a hasty meal and threw a lot of plaster etc. from the furniture. It was heart-breaking to see my own home so badly damaged after what I had been through.

I had to be back at the station by 5pm so I was unable to do any more at home. When darkness fell once again, there were at least a dozen fires still burning in the city. We had a warning again soon after dark and German bombers could be heard overhead, but no bombs were dropped. The German Air Force could have burned us to the ground that night had they dropped more incendiaries, as we had no water supply other than the Sherbourne, and it must have been possible to see Coventry miles away as fires were breaking out over a week later, and I remember in Broadgate on Christmas morning, over six weeks later, smoke could be seen rising over piles of bricks where shop walls had collapsed into cellars.

There were between five hundred and six hundred people killed in that raid of 13 hours. Thousands were rendered homeless and hundreds of thousands of pounds worth of damage done to buildings and property.

A lot of us policemen slept fully-clothed at the station for weeks after as we had nowhere to go. Conditions in Coventry were terrible after that raid for weeks. There was a shortage of food for a start until the Ministry of Food released a big consignment for Coventry, and rationing was suspended for a month. Water was the worst problem, some people having to carry it in buckets for miles. Some even boiled rainwater. Even this had to be done on a fire as there was no gas. Most districts had electricity by Christmas and I remember we had to cook mother's Christmas dinner on our electric stove as we had no gas.

For days after the raid, DA (delayed action) bombs were going off day and night, and a lot of people were killed by these, being unaware of their presence. No-one was allowed in the City unless on important business for weeks afterwards. Soldiers were leant to help clear the City, and dangerous buildings had to be blasted to make them safe.

On the 16th November the King visited the City, and after that nearly every well-known personage paid us a visit, from the P.M's (Prime Ministers) of Britain, Australia, and Canada downwards. We received world-wide sympathy, and an Air-raid Distress Fund was started to which thousands of pounds were subscribed.

One of the saddest scenes was the Communal Funeral of the victims who were buried together in one grave at the London Road Cemetery. No private funerals were allowed, dozens of people were buried unidentified.

The raid seemed to wake up the country to the danger of fire bombs, and groups of Fire Guards were formed, so it is unlikely that any town would ever experience such a raid again."

Wilfred was one of five children. His father Ernest was also in the Coventry City Police and was due to retire near the start of the War, but with manpower being limited due to men leaving to join the Armed Forces a block was put on retirements, so he ended up staying until he had reached 31 years' service.

Wilfred and Ernest during WWII, note the straps across their coats indicating they are carrying their gas masks on their backs

Wilfred's sister Olive did her part too: she was in the Home Guard. She participated in weekly activities and was trained in first aid, delivering essential medical services after air raids at designated first aid points. She also trained in self-defence and rifle shooting.

Wilfred joined the Royal Navy in August 1942, returning to the police at the end of 1945. He wasn't to stay long though: on 10 September 1947 he resigned and emigrated from Coventry to move across the world to Canada, initially joining the British Columbia Police. Within a year he had transferred to the Royal Mounted Police where he had a long and successful career, retiring on 30 December 1977.

With huge thanks to Wilfred's sister Olive and her son Roy for sharing these memories and pictures.

An officer peers into the road works. Note he carries his steel helmet in case of further raids. Is that a police messenger to his left? Picture Courtesy of David McGrory

There were other raids across the city but some respite must have been welcomed over winter when weather conditions for the Luftwaffe prevented them from flying.

The second heavy raid to mention took place on the 8 April 1941. The raid would last six hours and fifty minutes and would leave a further 281 dead. The police station in St Mary Street which had only suffered minor damage previously took a direct hit on this night resulting in the deaths of four officers and causing extensive damage to the station. On the following pages you can see the bombed out St Mary Street station – including the coat still hanging on the back of the office door. ©Alamy.

The officers that died in the bombing of St Mary Street are Special Constable Frank Henry Kimberley, Specials Commander Arthur Frederick Matts MBE, Special Constable Thomas Arthur Harraway and Special Constable Harold Leslie Lowe who was found the following day in the wreckage.

There was understandably confusion in the initial aftermath of the explosion in Coventry, with SC H J Pemberton being reported in the paper as being killed. It turned out he was only injured and found himself in the unique position of reading his own obituary.

Whilst all the auxiliary roles were important, and ensured policing in Coventry continued during the war, the police messenger role is one that is often overlooked. It is hard to imagine the bravery required of a police messenger: how a boy of 16 with nothing but a tin helmet and a push bike, was expected to cycle around and take messages to officers on the ground or between stations or emergency services during air raids; with no street lighting as the black-out was in place, bombs dropping around him, people screaming, fires all over the places, telephone poles and other street furniture blown apart and causing hazards, to give but a brief description of the worst of their shifts.

George Frederick Barrett is a shining example of the quality of police messenger in Coventry. His father, Frederick Barrett, had been a special constable and was killed during the devastating air raid in November 1940. Too young to follow in his father's footsteps as a special constable, he promptly became a police messenger. During one particular night, for which he received the British Empire Medal, George was inside a building that suffered a direct hit by a bomb and was 'blown by the blast for some distance.'[21] After recovering, he made his way to report to the main Air Raid Precautions (ARP) control centre and was sent out with his next message. On the way he was blown off his cycle by another blast. Not deterred, the young messenger got back on his bike and continued with his work. He then ran into some trouble when he cycled straight into some telephone wires that had come down, causing injuries to his neck – but he still continued and made sure to deliver the message safely, returning with the reply. After receiving some first aid, he continued to take more messages out that night.

Messenger Howard George Miles (18) also received the British Empire Medal – he 'rendered great assistance by delivering urgent and important messages. He dealt with many incendiary bombs, and at grave risk to himself, helped to rescue a baby who was trapped in the wreckage of a house.'[22]

Messenger Alfred Leslie Poretta (17) was another brave young man serving the Coventry City Police – during an air raid he was blown some distance by the blast of a bomb and although suffering from the effects, made his way through the debris to the ARP Control Room for more messages to deliver. He volunteered for one very urgent message for the casualty service during a particularly violent period of bombing, a message which took over an hour to deliver.

---

[21] Coventry Standard, 28 June 1941
[22] Coventry Standard, 28 June 1941

Left to right, Poretta, Miles and Barrett – receiving their medals at the Palace, 26 November 1941 from the Evening Dispatch (©Reach PLC)

Detective Superintendent Cyril George Boneham MM BEM

Cyril Boneham served for seven years with the Goldstream Guards during World War I and was awarded the Military Medal during his service. He joined Coventry City Police in 1920 and in 1938 succeeded Detective Chief Inspector Bowers as head of the force's CID, becoming their first Detective Superintendent.

He was reported to have rendered particularly fine service during the I.R.A. outrages in 1939 and in 1941 when St Mary Street was bombed, being awarded the British Empire Medal (along with Detective Inspector Edward Pendleton) for his part in rescuing 12 injured colleagues where he took great personal risk in assisting with their rescue. Several colleagues were of course killed in this blast and the rescue must have been particularly traumatic. On the same night, Cyril narrowly escaped being caught up in the bomb blast on Jordan Well that killed several of his colleagues. The officers were attempting to rescue people trapped in a cellar following bomb blasts earlier in the air raid. Cyril went back to the police station for help as the bombs continued to drop, when he heard the devastating sound of explosions nearby. When he returned to the cellar the occupants and the whole rescue party had been killed.

Pic ©Reach PLC

Cyril lost his first wife suddenly in December 1940 and as was common at the time, with two children to consider and a very demanding day job, re-married soon after in 1942. Sadly in 1943 she became seriously ill and on Sunday 10 January 1943 he was informed that she was dangerously ill. It was reported that Cyril had been suffering with his own ill-health problems for some time and after receiving the message from the hospital, that Sunday night in his office he shot and killed himself. His automatic service revolver was found near him, and two letters were found in his pocket – one to the Chief Constable and one to Detective Inspector Pendleton. It was reported at the inquest that they referred to his domestic troubles and said they were getting him down. The Chief Constable said at the inquest that Cyril had left behind a stainless character both professionally and as far as he knew, personally, stating that he was a staunch man of the highest integrity.

As a result of research for this book, Cyril's story was located and he has subsequently been added to both the West Midlands Police Roll of Honour and the National Police Roll of Honour. Recent changes to the inclusion criteria in line with a better understanding of mental health issues mean that suicides whilst on duty (even if not related to police duty) are now considered for addition, just as they are for deaths relating to other medical problems.

This fantastic picture shows members of the special constabulary, possibly a war reserve constable in the custodian helmet and a police messenger sitting at the front.

Prime Minister Winston Churchill visited Coventry in June 1945. This picture was taken as he addressed the crowds on June 25, on Trinity Street. PC Thomas Wilson, referred to earlier in this book in the Coventry Bobbies section, can be seen to the right of Churchill in uniform, with the number 1 prominent on his collar.

It has previously been reported that Churchill knew of the November 1940 raid in Coventry, prior to its occurrence, and was willing to let the city burn to ensure the Germans did not know about his secret intelligence sources. More recent articles, including one by Mr McIver, in Finest Hour 41, highlights that two of Churchill's former private secretaries have given clear accounts of the night of the raid – indicating that Churchill knew a big raid was coming, but mistakenly believed it was coming to London, and therefore additional precautions were taken in the capital, where no bombs were dropped that night.[23]

---

[23] https://winstonchurchill.org/resources/myths/churchill-let-coventry-burn/ accessed 3/5/2021

As previously mentioned, many officers were recalled to the Colours or volunteered to join the Armed Forces during World War II – sadly several of them did not return:

PC60 William Arthur Blower – Lance Corporal 2613418. 2nd Battalion, Grenadier Guards. Died in Belgium between Friday 31 May 1940 and Saturday 1 June 1940

William had previous service in the Mercantile Marines and Army prior to joining Coventry City Police. He was recalled to service and drafted to France before he took part in the withdrawal to the Channel Ports. William is buried in De Panne Communal Cemetery. He was 25 years of age.

PC 27 Edward Lloyd RATCLIFFE. Flying Officer 118621, 15 Squadron, Royal Air Force Volunteer Reserve. Died on sortie to Germany on Friday 19 February 1943.

Edward served as the navigator aboard a Stirling Mk. III bomber. His aircraft was shot down by Oberleutnant Joachim Jabs. The aircraft caught fire and exploded before crashing, killing the entire crew. Edward is buried in Ameland (Nes) General Cemetery in Grave D.13.17. He was 30 years of age and is commemorated on Rawmarch and Parkgate War Memorial, Rotherham.

PC 37 James CROMPTON. Ordinary Seaman D/JX 366348 H.M.S. "Kite", Royal Navy. Died at sea on Friday 4 June 1943.

On this date H.M.S Kite was transferred to offensive anti-submarine patrols in the Bay of Biscay to intercept U-Boats. During this period the British vessels were subjected to heavy air attacks and it is possible that James was killed during one such attack. James is commemorated on the Plymouth Naval Memorial on panel 80, column 2. He was 27 years of age.

PC 193 Douglas Cecil Blackford. Corporal 2695136 1st Battalion Scots Guards. Died in Italy on the 8 February 1944.

Corporal Blackford was killed at Anzio whilst his battalion was defending the factory and Correceto. Douglas was killed when he ignored an order to leave a comrade who was hit by a sniper – having been a police officer he was used to delivering first aid and went to assist. Tragically he himself was hit, sustaining 15 machine gun bullets and dying that day. The comrade he had helped, recovered from his wounds.

Douglas is buried in Beach Head War Cemetery, Anzio in Grave XX.D.11. He was 26 years of age.

PC 185 John William Smith. Sergeant (Air Gunner) 1583360 – RAF Volunteer Reserve. Died in Belgium on Friday 12 May 1944.

Aircraft serial number JB733 PM-K had taken off at 21:58 on 11/5/1944 from Elshom Wolds, and was shot down at Loenhout at 02:00 the next day. All but one of the crew had survived an accident in March that year.

Buried in grave IVa.D.3 at Schooselhof Cemetery in Belgium. He was 28 years of age.

PC 175 John Michael Arundel. Lieutenant 245224 3 Troop, 15th (Scottish) Regiment, Reconnaissance Corps, Royal Armoured Corps. Died in France on 10 July 1944

John was killed in action when his armoured car was struck by a tank shell, according to the War Diary, on Monday 10 July 1944. Lieutenant Arundel and his driver, Trooper Griffiths, were killed, though this was not confirmed for about 10 days.

He is buried in Banneville-La-Campagne War Cemetery in Grave IX.B.22. He was 33 years of age.

Kenneth William GREEN. Sergeant 14251832 "C" Squadron, Glider Pilot Regiment, Army Air Corps

Died in Holland on Tuesday 19/09/1944

Kenneth was involved in the landing of troops for operation Market Garden. Glider pilots having landed were joined fighting troops and fought alongside soldiers from various regiments. Kenneth has no known grave and is commemorated on the Groesbeek Memorial on Panel 8. He was 22 years of age. Kenneth hails from a 'police' family with his brother, Norman, and his nephew, Stephen, both serving in local police forces. His elder brother, Harry, served in the Royal Artillery.

PC 69 Sidney Alfred Taylor. Lance Bombardier 14251545 of the 76 Field Regiment, Royal Artillery.

Died on Sunday 15/10/1944.

Sadly no other details are known of how Sidney met his death. He is buried along with 276 other casualties in Overloon War Cemetery, grave IV.B.10 Netherlands. Sidney was 32 years of age.

PC 171 George William HOWLETT. Sergeant 5107689 Royal Warwickshire Regiment attached 2nd (Nyasaland) Battalion, 21st Brigade, King's African Rifles. Died in Kenya on Thursday 8 February 1945

Having had previous service with the Royal Warwickshire Regiment before joining Coventry City Police, George was recalled on reserve at the outbreak of war and was killed in a road accident.

He is buried in Nyeri European Roman Catholic Plot. He was later exhumed and reinterred in Nyeri War Cemetery in Grave 1.B.4 on Friday 22 March 1946.

PC 57 Sidney Thomas COOKE – Lance Corporal 14251494

8 Section, 110th Divisional Provost Company, Corps of Military Police. Died in Germany on Thursday 5 April 1945

Sidney was killed in an accident on a bridge.

He was initially buried in a temporary burial ground at Wallenhorst but was reinterred in Rheinberg War Cemetery in Grave 13.C.22 in January 1948. He was 28 years of age.

12. Coventry officers on the West Midlands Police Roll of Honour

Coventry City Police

Police Constable Reuben Needham Dickson

Died 17 November 1906 aged 52 - fatally injured when he fell off a set of ladders whilst cleaning the station windows. It was reported that Reuben was cleaning the windows when he leaned to the right and suddenly the ladder slipped and he fell, hitting some railings as he went. The Chief Constable reported that the force were quite devastated at his loss.

Police Sergeant James Arthur Fox

Killed 12 October 1940 aged 37 – Killed evacuating the area of a delayed action bomb in an air raid.

Police Constable William Henry Leedham

Killed 12 October 1940 aged 36 – killed evacuating the area of a delayed action bomb in an air raid.

Special Constable William Matson Sinclair

Killed 21 October 1940 aged 33 – killed during an enemy air raid.

Special Constable Harry Berry

Killed 14 November 1940 aged 34 – killed by enemy action when an air raid shelter was destroyed. When his brother was told of his death by one of Harry's colleagues the next day, he listened intently and said: "Officer, will you do me a favour? Please let me take my brother's place as a special constable."[24]

Police Constable Kenneth Charles Rollins

Killed 14 November 1940 aged 30 - killed by enemy action when trying to evacuate members of the public who had been trapped in a cellar during an air raid. Constable 25 Rollins was aged 30 and lived at 111 Sadler Road, with his wife Kathleen Annie. He was killed at Jordan Well shelter, the blast flung Kenneth over the wall of a local shop and colleagues were unable to save him from the fire. He was the son of a retired sergeant, Henry Rollins who finished his service in 1908. He died on 6th June 1939 at the age of 77 years. His wife Rosa Alice died in 1955 aged 92. Following the death of her husband she then lost her son Henry Reginald aged 45 years, who died after a short illness in Birmingham on 13th November 1940. The very next day Kenneth was killed by the German bombs. One year after the deaths of constables Timms and Rollins the City Police Band placed a memorial in the local newspapers remembering their two fallen colleagues, 'who died in the execution of their duty'

---

[24] Research by Ray Greenhow

Police Constable William Alfred Henry Timms

Killed 14 November 1940 aged 23 – killed by enemy action when trying to evacuate members of the public who had been trapped in a cellar during an air raid. Constable 82 Timms was only 23 years of age and in the electoral register of 1939 was listed as a constable; at the time of his death he was living at 51 Quinton Road, Coventry. It would be uncommon for a man of 23 years to make a will, but William had done so. Perhaps this was the expectation of risk through his policing role in a city that had already been bombed. He left £117 10s to his widowed mother Catherine Josephine Timms who lived at 48 Millers Road; She died in 1946 aged 52 years.[25]

Police Auxiliary Messenger Thomas Rowland Lowry

Killed 14 November 1940 aged 16 - killed by enemy action when an air raid shelter was destroyed. Thomas is the youngest person on the West Midlands Police Roll of Honour. The below information comes from research by Ray Greenhow for the National Police Roll of Honour Trust:

> 'One of the youngest people to ever be added to the Police National Roll of Honour was Thomas Roland Lowry, the youngest son of Richard and Alice Clare Lowry of 42 Gordon Street. He was too young to take a role in any form of civil defence other than the Police Messenger Service, so eagerly joined to play his part and was paid a wage of 28 shillings a week. He had been on duty at the Central Police Station when a communication arrived and had to be carried to Much Park. He tucked it into his pocket and disappeared into the moonlight to do his duty. He was killed by a bomb that fell on the Jordan Well air raid shelter that he was taking refuge in at the time.
>
> The family were poor and Thomas's earnings, minus a small amount of pocket money went to his mother to supplement his father's railway drayman's wage. Thomas's other brothers were in the Armed Forces, and he would look up to them. The family used to live in the poorer courts of Coventry that were let to tenants, but Alice had saved towards a deposit to obtain a better home for her family. Following Thomas's death, she had applied to the Ministry of Pensions under the Personal Injuries (Civilians) Pensions Scheme and was told one could not be granted unless her circumstances materially and permanently altered and was not just temporary.
>
> The pain of Thomas's death to Mrs Lowry could be seen in the Memorial columns of the local papers where notices appeared virtually every year beginning on 12th November 1941 with the following in quotation: "Sweet are the memories that never fade, of one we loved but could not save: our loss is great and will remain, until in heaven we meet again." They ended in

---

[25] Research by Ray Greenhow

November 1952 with the poignant words: "May his sacrifice bring peace and freedom, for which he died." In April 1953, notices were placed in the paper following the death of Thomas's father. On 24th December of that same year Alice passed away and a notice was also placed with the quotation, 'Peace after Pain'. No notice had been placed in the papers on Thomas's anniversary in November 1953; it may be that she was too ill. The pain referred to could have been caused by an ongoing illness, or that pain she had endured since 14th November 1940. Most likely it would be both, but finally, as wished for in the 1941 memorial, she was finally re-united in heaven with Thomas.'

Special Constable William Robert Lambe

Killed 14 November 1940 aged 26 – killed by enemy action trying to help others trapped in a shelter. William Robert Lambe was 26 years old and had come to Coventry from Belfast in 1935, joining the Special Constabulary at the outbreak of war. He was the son of a former Belfast councillor, his brother John still worked for the estates department of the Belfast Corporation. He worked as a fitter and lived with his wife Sarah and their daughter at Wycliffe Grove, Wyken. Both Sarah and their daughter were in Belfast at the time of the air attack. William died outside Jordan Well shelter, again trying to rescue others who were trapped. He left £214 13s 9d in his will to Sarah.

Special Constable Frederick Barratt

Killed 14 November 1940 aged 50 – killed by enemy action when an air raid destroyed the city centre. The below research is from Ray Greenhow for the National Police Roll of Honour Trust:

'Special Constable Frederick Barratt was 50 years of age and lived at 135 Poole Road, married to Florence and they are known to have had two sons and two daughters. He was a veteran of the Great War, and men of that conflict were now too old to serve again in the Armed Forces, although they still had a sense of duty to their nation when under threat. Frederick, a parks keeper, joined the Special Constabulary to play what part he could. He was injured by a bomb that fell at Lythalls Lane, Foleshill while he was on duty and was taken to the Coventry & Warwickshire hospital, dying the same day. Their son George Frederick was only 19 at the time but became a police messenger in the finest tribute he could pay to his father, to serve as Frederick had done. Florence lost her brave husband during that terrible night of bombing and came close to losing George Frederick in a further night of carnage for Coventry on 9th and 10th April 1941. Four more police personnel were killed that night; there was very nearly a fifth. George Frederick had only been a messenger for four months and was in a building when it received a direct hit from a bomb and he was blown some distance by the blast. When he recovered he reported to the main control centre and was sent out with a message to the Allesley First Aid Post. He was

blown off his cycle by another bomb blast, recovered, remounted and continued with his duty. A telegraph line had fallen, and he rode into the wires, receiving neck injuries 6 inches in length that required treatment. He then finished his delivery, returning with the reply, then continued to deliver new messages as the bombs continued to rain down on the city. He was awarded the British Empire Medal for his bravery; had his father been alive he would have burst with pride. The tradition at a marriage is of a daughter being given away by her father to her husband-to-be, but that could not be so for Frederick and Florence's second daughter Norma. However, George Frederick Barratt, B.E.M., performed the role of his father at Holy Trinity Church, Coventry on Saturday 22nd September 1951.'

Special Constable Albert Ernest Bawden

Killed 14 November 1940 aged 38 – killed by enemy action when an air raid destroyed the city centre. His brave actions were recognised in awards bestowed on the heroes of the blitz, many posthumously including Albert's 'Kings Commendation for Brave Conduct in Civil Defence'. He was a partner in a firm of decorators but fulfilled his duty to his community as a special constable of Coventry's Specials B Division. On that fateful night of 14th November, he went out time after time in the most dangerous of circumstances. While driving in Newdigate Road he crashed into a bomb crater and another bomb fell close by, and he was seriously injured. He was taken to Coventry and Warwickshire hospital where he died that day. His wife Florence only lived a further 9 months, dying on 4th August 1941 at the age of 36; the family notice in the papers announcing her death finished succinctly yet poignantly with, 'Reunited'. Albert's mother was formerly Elizabeth Berry, the sister to Herbert Berry. Herbert was Special Constable Harry Berry's father, so both he and Albert were cousins and died together on the same night, albeit at separate incidents.[26]

Police Auxiliary Messenger Bertram Whyatt West

Injured 14 November 1940 when an air raid destroyed the city centre. He died the following day in Coventry and Warwickshire Hospital, aged 17. He lived with his parents at 50 Wheelwright Lane, Coventry and was an apprentice engineer. He would be supplementing his wage with a police auxiliary messenger service role. He was seriously injured on the night of the 14th at Hollbrooks Lane, Coventry and died on the 15th at Coventry and Warwickshire Hospital.[27]

---

[26] Research by Ray Greenhow
[27] Research by Ray Greenhow

Police War Reserve Constable Frederick Solomon Strong

Injured 14 November 1940 when enemy action destroyed the city centre. He died three days later on the 17th in Warwick Hospital aged 34. Police War Reserve Constable Frederick Solomon Strong lived with his wife Elsie, at 43 Gorseway, Coventry. He was seriously injured at the rear of 37 Gorseway and died at Warwick hospital on 17th, his death being recorded in that area. It is likely that the injured would be distributed to nearby hospitals to assist the Coventry and Warwickshire hospital that would have been unable to cope with the huge casualty list.[28]

Special Constable Frank Kimberley

Killed 8 April 1941 aged 54 – killed during an air raid when the police station on St. Mary Street suffered a direct hit.

Police War Reserve Constable Thomas Arthur Harraway

Killed 9 April 1940 aged 63 – killed during an enemy air raid on the police station on St. Mary Street Coventry

Special Commandant Arthur Frederick Matts M.B.E.

Injured 8 April 1941 when the police station in St. Mary Street was bombed in an enemy air raid. He died the following day on 9 April aged 48, at Warwick Hospital. Matts was awarded his MBE because of his devotion to duty during the blitz, and the fact he put himself on duty during every air raid, commanding the special constabulary during those dark nights.

[28] Research by Ray Greenhow

Special Constable Harold Leslie Lowe

Killed 10 April 1941 aged 37 – killed in an enemy air raid when the police station on St. Mary Street suffered a direct hit.

Warwickshire & Coventry Constabulary

Police Constable Peter Guthrie QPM

The first officer to be killed in Coventry since the 2nd World War – Peter was shot dead on the 28 July 1972 aged 21 trying to arrest a suspect who had broken into a gun shop. Posthumously awarded the Queen's Police Medal for Gallantry. Whilst Peter was serving with Warwickshire and Coventry Constabulary at the time of his death, his name is recorded on the West Midlands Police Roll of Honour as he is very fondly remembered in Coventry by members of the former Coventry City Police and of the later West Midlands Police.

West Midlands Police

Several Coventry officers have sadly been lost following the formation of West Midlands Police in 1974:

PC Phillip Mark Sanderson - Killed in a patrol car crash while responding to an assistance call - aged 20, 10 August 1978

DC Alexander Lawton Hamilton Forrest took ill and died whilst policing an election meeting, initially refusing to leave his post after feeling unwell, aged 45, 24 April 1979

PC Joseph Anthony O'Brien was fatally injured when struck by a car while directing traffic in a road race - aged 48, 14 November 1982

PC Gavin Richard Carlton was killed in the line of duty back on 19 December 1988. Gavin chased offenders who had robbed the Midland Bank in his police car, but after they shot at his car he mounted the pavement and became stuck on a bollard. As he tried to reverse his car away the callous offenders shot him at point blank range before driving away. After being confronted by other officers from the CID, following a car chase, foot chase and a second car chase, they were eventually caught. One turned his gun on himself and the other was sentenced to 14 years imprisonment for armed robbery. Gavin was 29 years old.

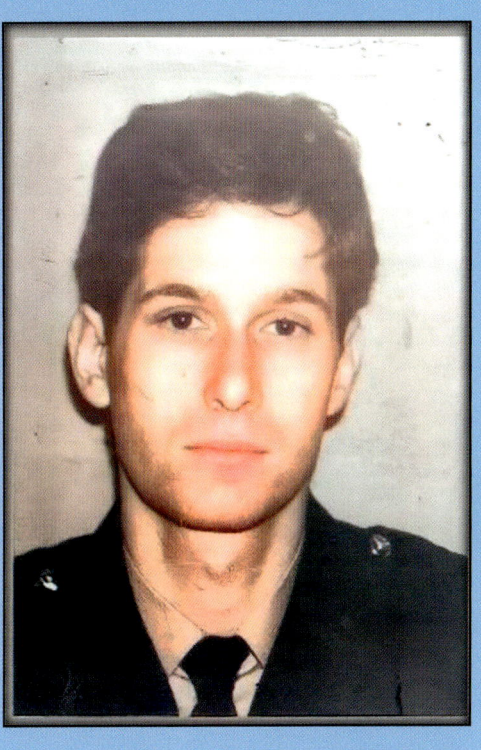

PC Mark John Woodhead collapsed and died whilst on duty at Fletchamstead Police Station on 26 January 1992, aged 32

PC Deborah Adele Harman-Burton Whilst not working in Coventry at the time of her death, Deborah was formerly a Coventry officer. She was killed in a road accident whilst travelling home from night duty - aged 28 – on 24 March 2006

13. Police Dogs

Police dogs were introduced to Coventry in 1961, only a few years after the regional dog training centre was set up in Stafford. Retired PC Bob Haynes has shared the below information and pictures on the history of police dogs in Coventry:

The three officers shown above were, left to right, P.C. Gavin "Jock" Archibald with P.D. Flame; P.C. Ron Freail with P.D. Blaze, and P.C. Ron Owen with P.D. Dante. They were the first three dog handlers and police dogs in Coventry in 1961.

These three officers attended the newly formed Regional Police Dog Training Centre at Stafford. There they were given their new dogs and completed a 13 week course. When they returned to Coventry and took up operational duties they had many challenges to overcome. They very much had to prove their worth.

Purely from a dog training point of view they were very much on their own, the nearest "experts" were at the Regional School 50 miles away, and their experience had been accrued over little more than a handful of years! It was very much a case of trial and error. Remember, the dog training world that we all know and enjoy, did not exist then. There was not the multitude of training clubs and professional trainers that we know now. It is thanks to these three men and others like them all over the country, that dog training in general, and professional dog training in particular, progressed as it did.

The decision for the naming of the dogs with names connected to fire lay with the Chief Constable at that time, E.W.C. (Ted) Pendleton. He, like all Coventrians, remembered only too well that less than twenty years earlier the city had been heavily bombed by the German air force and parts had been literally burnt to the ground. He felt that the naming of his police dogs should serve as a remembrance to the Blitz.

This tradition carried on some months later when demand for the services of police dogs was continually growing, and a decision was made to appoint another three handlers. These officers and their dogs are shown on the below photo which was taken at the annual inspection of the Force by H.M. Inspector of Constabulary. On the front row are the three originals and on the second row are P.C. Gordon Semmons with P.D. Flash. P.C. Alan Jennings with P.D. Firey, and P.C. Sidney Price with P.D. Flint:

Within another year they were followed by P.C. Peter Champs with P.D. Red and P.C. Bill Jessiman with P.D. Blitz. This tradition of giving the dogs names that were connected with fire then died out but was to some degree resurrected in the 1970s and 1980s when a keen young dog handler with a strong sense of history came on the scene and during this period handled both P.D. Dante and P.D. Flint!

With thanks to retired PC Bob Haynes for the information and pictures.

14. Vehicles

Motorcycle patrols were an important part of policing prior to panda cars being introduced, helping officers to cover more ground and react swiftly to incidents. The below picture shows a motorcycle patrol during World War II, likely to be early Triumph Speed Twins, probably 500cc as designed by Edward Turner just pre-war. They would have been built at the factory in Coventry but this was bombed during the war and a new one was built at Meriden.

One of the early patrol cars used in Coventry was the Humber Hawk: also pictured on the front cover, below it is parked outside Little Park Street Police Station in the early 1960s. The female officer is WPC Thelma Riley. Bottom of page: the Humber fleet is inspected.

Two Humber Hawks on the left, followed by two Hillman Minx's and possibly a Hillman Husk on the far right – and is that Edward Pendleton handing something over to the other gentleman in civilian clothing? Could this be an inspection of vehicles prior to placing an order...?

This picture shows Ginger Perkins and Charlie Smith posing with a Sunbeam Talbot 90, with thanks to Ginger's son John

Below is PC Martin Joseph Mullaney with the Hillman Imp Panda car: the Coventry based Rootes group was directed to manufacture the Imp at a plant in Linwood, Scotland. With many parts and components manufactured in the Midlands, these had to be transported some 300 miles to be assembled Linwood before being returned to a garage in Coventry. The Rootes Stoke factory which built and tested the engines ironically employed six Coventry special constables, who were able to play a part in production of the vehicles. The Hillman Imp was the first 'panda' patrol car to be used in the city, arriving ready for deployment on 1 April 1968, after being trialled throughout March. The fleet of 26 cars enabled the force to cover much more ground across the suburbs of Coventry and changed policing the city forever with the introduction of Unit Beat Policing.

Superintendent E Norton outlined their six-point panda plan[29]:

1. To increase police efficiency
2. Cultivate a better police-public understanding by bringing a closer contact between the public and the man on the beat and give a swifter response to calls for help and in dealing with complaints
3. Increase and improve the flow of information
4. Overcome the shortage of police officers by combining resources
5. Create new challenge in the method of beat working
6. Stimulate interest among members participating in the scheme by placing more responsibility upon individual officers

He further explained: *'If the scheme is to achieve its aims, we will need great co-operation from members of the public. We want to encourage them to look to the Panda cars for help, and pass on information - however small - which may assist in enquiries into crime and other incidents.*

All our drivers have received training in one of these cars and periodical refresher courses will be given.

Emergency calls will be answered even more efficiently than at present, because a Panda car will always be within a few minutes' driving distance.

There are bound to be teething troubles at first because the system is new. But we hope Coventry will have an even more efficient Police Force than at present.'

The fleet of Hillman Imps at Little Park Street Police Station – Coventry Evening Telegraph 28th March 1968, ©Reach PLC

---

[29] https://british-police-history.uk Spring 2021 journal

Only the City Centre was left out of the new unit system (as it was left to conventional foot patrols) and the cars were to be on patrol for 24 hours a day, with five drivers allocated per car. Each car would also be used by a detective and a policewoman.

A former salesman from the Rootes Group got in touch with British Police History recently and gave them the following information about Hillman Imps:

'The Imp engine as a matter of interest had an all-aluminium block which was quite revolutionary at the time for a small production car.

The engine was based on the famous Coventry Climax racing engine and, during pre-production trials at Ryton in the early 60's, the car was found to be far too fast so the engine was de-tuned to two thirds to comply with certain regulations at the time.

However, the Imp did have one ongoing mechanical problem which is why I'm slightly surprised the car was used by the police.

Because the engine was rear mounted, the throttle cable ran the whole length of the car from the accelerator pedal at the front all the way back to the carburettor in the rear. The cable had to negotiate several 'turns' on the way from front to back with obvious rubbing on metal parts.

The result was that the Imp was notorious for using an excessive number of throttle cables and I always carried a couple of spare ones in my company car! On one occasion just outside Swindon the cable broke as I was overtaking another vehicle which is not ideal!'

Panda cars also allowed for another innovation: around the time the cars were introduced, the Coventry City Police became the first force in the country to use miniature battery-operated tape recorders. Panda drivers dictated all reports of incidents witnessed or dealt with on to tapes, which were transcribed by staff back at the station, and passed back to the officer for signing.

'Each machine weighed only 6lb and was encased in steel and fitted with a leather carrying case with a shoulder strap. The dictating machines, costing £58 each were developed to the specifications of the Coventry Force and eighteen were delivered, one for each of the operational Panda cars.

Before all of the new Panda cars took to the roads of Coventry's suburbs all of the drivers received training in the use of the machines from staff of the manufacturer'[30].

PC Mullaney using the dictaphone

Superintendent Neville Chamberlain, head of the Force's administration department had this to say about the machines:

'We asked the firm to provide robust machines because they will undoubtedly have to stand any amount of wear and tear.

---

[30] British Police History Journal - Spring 2021, from Coventry Evening Telegraph 22/3/1968

Alterations were made to the machines originally supplied, and they now seem most satisfactory. Dictating will be done, whenever possible, in cars. It is not economic to have police officers sitting in offices writing or typing reports. By using these recorders we will be able to keep the men on the road where they can serve the rate-payers.

When the initial problems are ironed out the machines will help us to provide a more modern police force. They will enable the Panda team - of driver, Detective and Policewoman - to be a self-contained unit.'[31]

By the 1970s the force had moved to Austins: pictured here are an Austin Mini and Austin Allegro during the mid-1970s

---

[31] British Police History Journal – Spring 2021 from Coventry Evening Telegraph 22/3/1968

15. Diversity

The Daar Brothers

On the 16 March 1966 Mohamed Yusuf Daar (known as Joe) made history when he joined Coventry City Police, becoming the first Asian (and probably the first Muslim) officer in the country. Previously an inspector in the police in Tanganyika, he came to the UK when Tanganyika gained independence (becoming Tanzania) as he did not want to lose his British citizenship. A new, more diverse future was coming for British policing when the decision was made to allow non-white applicants to apply to become police officers. The Chief Constable of Coventry City Police (Edward Pendleton) at the time had appeared on TV stating that there would soon be 'coloured police officers on the streets.' The next day Joe walked into Little Park Street Police Station and joined up.

He has recalled how he received letters from all over the world after his story featured in the press – including one from Mauritius which was addressed simply to PC Daar – England!

Joe felt that he could do a lot of good supporting other BME officers, but the other elements to the role were not for him so after two years he left the police.

Joe's legacy does not stop there – with his brother Yunus also being inspired to join the police in Coventry in 1968.

Sgt Yunus Daar - pictured

Yunus remained with the police for 14 years and stated that his ethnicity was never an issue – even when he married a white colleague, he states he only experienced gossip, never any negativity. One particular incident he recalled was when he was in the back of a police van with a group of colleagues when the conversation turned to racism, prejudice and the challenges police officers face. Yunus then said something and everyone suddenly went quiet. He was worried he had said the wrong thing but one of the other officers then apologised and said they kind of forgot that he was there, they were talking about racism and prejudice from a white perspective and hadn't even considered that he was not 'one of them'. For Yunus, this confirmed his belief that ethnicity and colour did not matter and that he was part of a team with his colleagues. He achieved promotion to the rank of inspector before he left to go and work with his brother Joe.

The Daar brothers, pictured in 2016 (Yunus – left, and Joe – right)

Both Daar brothers are proud of how their family have contributed to policing and are pleased whenever they see a senior black or Asian officer on the TV, which makes them see how far the service has progressed.

Karen King

Karen King was the first black female officer to serve in Coventry, and has shared her story below:

> I joined West Midlands Police in 1978 as a Police Cadet. In October 1979 when I was 18 and a half years old which was the youngest you could be, I joined as a regular Police officer and attended Ryton on Dunsmore Police training centre.
>
> I started off based at Fletchamstead Highway Police Station, Canley and was there as a uniformed response officer for 12 years, becoming a fast response driver having passed my advanced driving course.

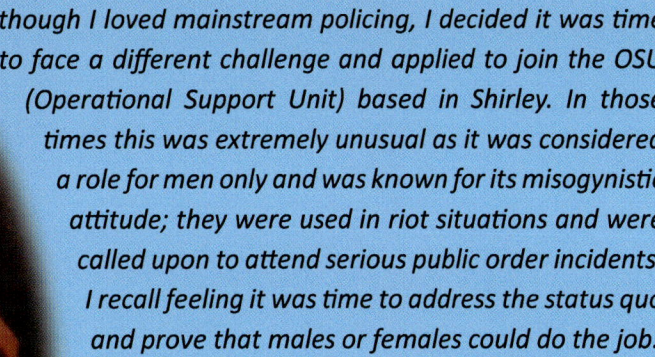

Although I loved mainstream policing, I decided it was time to face a different challenge and applied to join the OSU (Operational Support Unit) based in Shirley. In those times this was extremely unusual as it was considered a role for men only and was known for its misogynistic attitude; they were used in riot situations and were called upon to attend serious public order incidents. I recall feeling it was time to address the status quo and prove that males or females could do the job.

I recall turning up at Shirley, Solihull and the building where they were based had NO female showers so they had to put a lock on it for when I was in there. As you can imagine all of the Operational Support Officers were male and at first they were walking around on egg shells so as not to cause me any 'offence'. I found out later that the Sgt had given them a stern warning 'not to indulge in any traditional behaviour' towards new recruits that usually involved them being imprisoned in the dog kennel which was a standard 'welcome'.

I spent around 18 months there during which I passed my Sgts and Inspectors exam (at a time when you could study for and take both as a PC). I had a very rewarding time on the OSU and once they got to know me, they relaxed somewhat. I think they realised that even as a female the job could still be done.

When I left there - my legacy was a brand new female shower installed for future females and I hope, a message to other females not to be put off by 'what has gone before' or be restricted by a 'females can't do this' attitude.

I applied for promotion to Sgt and was successful, getting promoted around 1992. I was posted to Stechford Police Station. I spent approximately two years there and then went to Solihull as a uniformed response Sergeant. After two years or so I joined the Professional Standards Department (PSD) at West Midlands Police HQ.

During this posting I was promoted to Inspector around 1998 and became one of the first black female Inspectors in the West Mids, in fact I believe I WAS the first! This was a massive achievement to me as it was at a time when there were very few female officers being promoted to more senior ranks, many females I had initially joined with had left for various reasons, usually following having a family. Again, back then it was common for females to have a baby and be forced to leave as there was virtually no support or efforts to retain them as there are now.

I was in the PSD until 2006 when I returned to Coventry (back where I started off, so had come full circle), and became a uniformed neighbourhood inspector in Foleshill, Radford and Holbrooks.

I retired after exactly 30 years in 2009.

In 2010 I joined British Transport Police as a uniformed police Inspector (part time) and worked in their control room. In 2015 I became a uniformed response Inspector based at Birmingham

New St and that is where I still am, in uniform, fully operational, still keeping up the PST (personal safety training) at nearly 60!

I am married to Mel, also an ex WMP Officer who retired but now works as police support staff still with WMP. We have 3 fantastic children (whom I blame for me not getting promoted to above the rank of Inspector!!!!).

There were MANY challenges joining in 1979, both as a female and as a black female. I was also very young so that alone went against me. There was a fair bit of overt racism but my approach was to rise above it, to do my job and where necessary challenge it head on. Some of this came from other police officers who when challenged about casual racist comments would always say 'but we don't mean you Karen, you're one of us'. I like to think I maintained the balance of doing what was right with a touch of humour too and the vast majority of people I worked with were brilliant.

There are obvious changes between then and now, I recall when I first met my husband (early 80's) you had to apply to the superintendent of your station to live together whilst not married. I think I still have his type writer written reply, 'Permission granted, but should this way of life bring discredit to the Police Force, one of you will be required to move out'. It sounds archaic but the Police Force then was strict and very conservative in its approach.

The Force has changed of course, mainly in that these days EVERYTHING you do is captured on social media whereas in the 70s and 80s there were no phone cameras/CCTV/tech watching your every move. Attitudes have also changed and the Police have definitely become more diverse.

In conclusion, I LOVE this job, I knew I wanted to be a police officer from the age of 11, I lived with my Mum and 2 sisters in a single parent family, I grew up in a very poor neighbourhood in Coventry but most of us did to be fair. I credit my Mum for encouraging me to become a police officer and refusing to entertain the thought that it was not a job for someone with my background or ethnicity.

I have never regretted it and the only thing I sometimes fantasise about is not getting promoted to superintendent.....but having 3 kids between the ages of 2 and 8 during my 30s put paid to that!!

Karen in 2020

Karen wrote the above for us in 2020 and retired in May 2021, after being compulsorily retired upon reaching age 60.

16. Police Horses

It is unclear when Coventry first had police horses, but we have a selection of images that show them proudly patrolling the city – including an image of Chief Constable William Imber on horseback earlier in this book.

The below image was taken 4 April 1989 and shows police horses in the Upper Precinct. It is apparent that police horses ceased to be a part of Coventry City Police at some point and only returned upon amalgamation into West Midlands Police in 1974, when they were re-introduced to the city.

17. Police Boxes

West Midlands Police Museum have recently acquired a police box which is being restored so it can be displayed in the museum for people to get a better understanding of what they were like to work in.

Below is an account of police boxes by former Coventry PC Ray Starkey who retired in 1994, pictured here in his West Midlands Police uniform:

'I worked from a police box in Earlsdon between 1965 and 1968. Seven Beat had a box in Earlsdon Street and Eight Beat a box in Bristol Road.

When you joined, you were given a box key which opened all the police boxes in Coventry.

Parading On

At the start of your shift you were expected to arrive at the box 15 minutes early. This gave you time to look-up your parading-on point. This was a table of different street locations on the beat where, at your start time, you must be. Sometimes you would get a visit from a patrol sergeant who would formally "parade you on". This visit would be recorded in your pocketbook and countersigned by the sergeant.

You were supposed to walk to your parading on point but, if you were late, some of us rode our pedal cycles to it and hid them before the sergeant turned up.

(Police box in use in Bishop Street shown in the bottom left of the picture below)

Documents

In the box there was a tall stool and a built-in elevated table. The top was hinged and when you lifted it up you would find copies of the Police Gazette and Midland Crime Information. There was also a beat-book in which you recorded minor nuisances reported to you on patrol. It was your job to review the book and then patrol the areas where there appeared to be a problem.

The Floor

The floor in the boxes on 7 and 8 beats were wooden. The box in Earlsdon Avenue South near Kenilworth Road (Six box) had a concrete floor, the remains of which I believe are there to this day – although I haven't looked for ages.

Cleaning

The constable on the early shift on Sunday mornings had the job of sweeping the floor and making the box tidy. Officially there was no smoking in the box, but you only had to look around the walls to see the tar stains and to know that the rule was routinely broken.

When you sat at the desk there was a transom window in front of you. The smokers always opened it in case the inspector visited the box in which case the cigarette was thrown out of the window. Folk lore said it was the best store of fag-ends on the beat and the worst fire hazard!

Ringing-In

Each box had a public telephone which connected to the switchboard at Canley Police Station. You were expected to call in every hour and tell the operator where you were going for the next hour and which streets you would be walking. Sometimes you would be sent to a job but, in the main, the patrol car or police van answered calls for service. If you were late for a call the sergeant would be sent to find you.

Route-Book

You had to enter your route for the next hour in the route-book so that if the sergeant came to the box he could find you. This practice was discontinued around 1968 when personal radios appeared.

Circular routes were frowned on as were routes that used alleyways. Sergeants, forever suspicious, thought you might be malingering in a tea-spot and using the alleyways to miss out parts of your route. Earlsdon has lots of alleyways and some good tea-spots!

None of the boxes were heated and on nights when the temperature dropped below -10 centigrade you had a job writing your route as the ink in your biro would freeze up.

You quickly learned the road names when writing in the route-book.

Door-Slamming

As a young officer I fell afoul of Inspector 'Pip' Orange who found me coming out of the box in the early hours and slamming the Eight Box door behind me. I was given a double-quick dressing down, Second-World War style, about upsetting the neighbours. I got a second one from Pip in Queensland Avenue (near 8 box) months later when I slammed the patrol car door, again in the early hours. I never did that again.

Men like Inspector Orange were the best thing we had in Coventry Police. Most of them had two rows of campaign medals from 1939-45. They knocked us youngsters into shape – lessons that made us better men and better policemen. I am forever in his debt.

Ray Starkey

With thanks to Ray Starkey who has brought the memory of police boxes to life far better than we ever could. Pictured above rekindling his memory of police boxes Coventry Transport Museum.

Here retired police officers Mick Ross and Steve Rice prepare to disassemble the police box that was donated to the West Midlands Police Museum. The box stands in-front of a garage painted the same black colour (in case you thought it was that big!). Its roof is the smaller triangle shape.

Whilst it was still standing decades after being placed in the garden of a retired officer, it was in very poor condition with much of the external timber rotted away and the door altogether missing. The interior survived pretty well though, and you can see inside the desk which would be similar to the one given in Ray's account.

18. A lifetime of policing Coventry...

Gordon Meredith GM is a name many who have policed in Coventry will be familiar with. The 1983 issue of West Midlands Police magazine The Beacon details Gordon's career when commemorating his retirement:

Sgt Meredith joined the former Coventry City Police as a cadet in 1948 and was conscripted for National Service in 1950, enlisting in the Royal Corps of the Military Police. He reached the rank of corporal and was discharged from the Army and re-joined Coventry City Police in November 1952. He became sergeant in October 1961.

In July 1972 he responded to a call of a man breaking into a shop. The first officer on the scene was PC Peter Guthrie who was shot and killed at point blank range by a shotgun. Sergeant Meredith was next on the scene and, despite being shot in the thigh, struggled with the gunman and kept hold of the gun. The killer escaped but was later arrested and Gordon was awarded the George Medal for his bravery.

As a Federationist of many years standing, he rose to national prominence to become a member of the Joint Central Committee and the Police Negotiating and Police Advisory Boards and Chairman of the West Midlands Police Joint Branch Board.

One of Gordon's four children, Andrew, followed in his father's footsteps and became an officer with West Midlands Police, also stationed in Coventry. After two years as a cadet and a further 30 as a regular officer, Sergeant Meredith retired in December 1982. During his police career he sat on many different boards and served a great many roles alongside his Federation commitments, including being a trustee of the Gurney Fund for six years, a member of the Central Selection Board (Special Course), conducting graduate interviews and being a governor of the Police Staff College at Bramshill to name a few.

But his commitment to the police in Coventry did not end with his retirement – Gordon became a member of the Coventry branch of the National Association of Retired Police Officers (NARPO) and is currently their President.

Gordon (standing left) with Chief Constable Pendleton (right).

Speaking to Gordon recently, he told of some of the highlights of his policing career – including a visit to Cincinnati to represent the Board of Trade, sent by Coventry City Police. When asked what he thought had changed the most during his service – he was quick to comment on the introduction of panda cars and how they changed beat policing forever; removing officers from the street and putting them behind the wheel of a car. One of the most memorable incidents of his career was being one of the first on scene when IRA member James McDade was killed by a bomb he was planting in 1974. He witnessed absolute chaos and was placed in charge of the scene through the initial response.

19. Police Buildings

Many different buildings have been used to police Coventry, from the original Watch House building and the first police station in Market Place to Coventry Central Police Station on Little Park Street.

A picture of a model showing the Watch House was included at the beginning of this booklet and we also referenced the fact that the stocks were removed from the Watch House and placed outside the front of the police station in 1840. The picture below then, from Coventry Police Museum, may show the police station to the right?

St Mary Street Police Station opened in 1899 and was the main Coventry Police Station until 1957. After suffering extensive damage during World War II it was rebuilt and continued as the main headquarters for the force in 1957 when the new station opened on Little Park Street. Picture over the page:

Aside from St Mary Street, one of the oldest stations that can be recalled in Coventry is Holmsdale Road, Foleshill: pictured below (with thanks to Kevin Watson)

Many different beat and sector offices have existed in Coventry over the years, including Hillfields, William Malcolm House, Tarquin Road, Everdon Road, Wyken Sector, Stoke Aldermoor, Smithford Way Kiosk, Wood End, Hawkesbury, Tile Hill, George Poole House and Radford.

One location that brings back fond memories for former Coventry police officers, is 2 box – a small space to allow the public to talk to the police and also ensuring officers had a place to go to get in from the cold and take a quick break, just big enough for someone to sit and a toilet and a phone:

Other key stations in Coventry that are still in use by the force today include Coventry Central on Little Park Street:

Willenhall (below) formerly known as Chace Avenue Police Station:

Foleshill (formerly known as Stoney Stanton) Police Station:

Rear of Foleshill showing an unusual police sign:

Canley (formerly known as Fletchamstead) Police Station:

There is also a small sector office in Bell Green that is currently in use by West Midlands Police, made up of portakabins:

20.   Police Forces of Coventry

Coventry City Police 1836 – 1969

Warwickshire & Coventry Constabulary 1969 – 1974

West Midlands Police 1974 - today

Canley (formerly known as Fletchamstead) Police Station:

There is also a small sector office in Bell Green that is currently in use by West Midlands Police, made up of portakabins:

20.   Police Forces of Coventry

Coventry City Police 1836 – 1969

Warwickshire & Coventry Constabulary 1969 – 1974

West Midlands Police 1974 - today

21. Coventry City of Culture

'My name is Chief Inspector Helen Kirkman and I am the policing lead for City of Culture in West Midlands Police.

I have worked in Coventry for a number of years and have a real love of the city. Coventry has so much to offer, and when the chance to work on City of Culture came about I jumped at it. I wanted to be involved in something special that would bring Coventry into the spotlight. To showcase all the aspects that make it a great place to be while shining a light on Coventry's amazing people.

West Midlands Police is excited and proud to be an official delivery partner as part of City of Culture. We are working with the City of Culture Trust, the City Council and many partners to make the year the best it can be.

From a policing perspective, we are involved in City of Culture for many reasons, but all the reasons are underpinned by us working to make Coventry a safer city for all who live, work and visit here.

West Midlands Police have been involved in the planning from an early stage. The more traditional side of our work is working with partners on planning for the events that will take place during the year and this will ensure that the events, activities and city are safe, and that everyone attending them or visiting the city can enjoy them.

However, City of Culture presents a unique opportunity for Coventry and West Midlands Police want to be part of something that helps create genuine change in Coventry.

This is where the more innovative side of our involvement is working to see how we can use arts and culture to reduce crime, focus on our safety priorities such as youth violence or domestic abuse.

We also want to connect with communities, build trust and protect vulnerable people. For different reasons we understand that we do face times when people feel that they don't want to talk to us or work with us. There will be new and different ways to have conversations with members of the public during the year and we will use these to develop closer links and build trust.

Lastly, we want to make sure our work creates a legacy longer than just the title year by showcasing what a great place getting involved with West Midlands Police voluntarily or through a career can be.

It is very exciting to have City of Culture taking place. It's a chance to celebrate our city and to show the world how we can bounce back after difficult times such as the pandemic. I am excited to be part of this incredible opportunity and determined West Midlands Police will do all it can to ensure the City of Culture year is a success.'